"Normal"
Isn't coming back
But Jesus is!

A book about the Return of Jesus Christ

(Yeshua Hamashiach)

What you should know about the different Raptures

Scriptures on Baptism, Salvation, and the Holy Spirit

And more!

Written by

Courtney Lande

If we are not nearing the end, I hope to be writing more!

We were told to occupy until Jesus Christ

(Yeshua Hamashiach) comes so that is what I'm doing!

Thank you to all who purchased this book!

Upcoming Future Books:

"Normal"

isn't coming back

But Jesus is!

"You Live

And

You Learn"

A special Selection of Poems

Courtney Lande has written over the years

Throughout her Life

and

A Portrait of Her as a Person

Trials

Tribulations

To

Triumph!

An Autobiography

Of Courtney Lande's testimony

My story so far:

Giving God all Glory Honor and Praise

For the Miracles in my Life

Philippians 2: 8-11 ⁸ And being found in fashion as a man, he humbled himself, and became obedient unto death, even the death of the cross. ⁹ Wherefore God also hath highly exalted him, and given hiem a name which is above every name: ¹⁰ That at the name of Jesus every knee should bow, of things in heaven, and things in earth, and things under the earth; ¹¹ And that every tongue should confess that Jesus Christ is Lord, to the glory of God the Father.

Titus 2:13 ¹³ Looking for that blessed hope, and the glorious appearing of the great God (Yahweh) and our Messiah, Lord and savior Jesus Christ (Yeshua Hamashiach).

Revelation 1:7 ⁷ Behold, He is coming with clouds and Every eye will see him, even they who pierced Him, and all kindreds of the earth shall wail because of him. Even so, Amen.

1 Corinthians 10: 31 [31]" Whether therefore you eat, or drink, or whatsoever you do, do all to the glory of God!"

Contents

The chapters are categorized by the soul expression of the author, Courtney Lande.

Chapters

Happy Resurrection Day! 2026

Hi everyone!

For those who don't know me, my name is Courtney Lande. I'm a gal who has an ardent passion to spread the Gospel and love of Jesus Christ; as the majority of the world recognizes Him as Jesus Christ, His real name is Yeshua Hamashich. I use both names interchangeably when talking about Jesus Christ (Yeshua Hamashiach) as that is how most people refer to Him. It brings me great joy when I read His words found in the Bible. I personally own many and like reading from the King James Bible. I do not have a degree in theology or ministry, and I am not a pastor, preacher, or minister. I find joy in reading and researching Scriptures from the King James Bible as I follow along with pastors who teach directly from the word of God (Yahweh). To the best of my knowledge, I will provide Scriptures from the King James Version Edition to back up my findings in this book.

Chapter 1
The purpose and impact Jesus Christ (Yeshua Hamashiach) has on humanity

What an impact Jesus Christ (Yeshua Hamashiach) has on humanity!

Jesus Christ (Yeshua Hamashiach) of Nazareth is the Messiah, the divine Son of the living God, conceived of the Holy Spirit, born in human flesh of the virgin Mary, who died on the cross for our sins, was buried, and on the third day rose again. He sits at the right hand of the Father (Yahweh) as our High Priest and Advocate. It was an incredible act of selflessness and service when Jesus Christ (Yeshua Hamashiach) sacrificed Himself, taking on the punishment for our sins and sicknesses, in His body dying on the cross for all. He sacrificed Himself on the cross so that we might die to sin and live for righteousness. We are saved by grace through faith in the finished work of Jesus Christ (Yeshua Hamashiach). It's not by any works we do, lest any man should boast. Our salvation is found in Him alone. The moment we believe and put our faith and trust in Jesus Christ (Yeshua Hamashiach), the moment we make Him our personal Lord and Savior, we are saved and justified by the blood of Jesus (Yeshua). It is having an intimate relationship with Jesus Christ (Yeshua Hamashiach), birthed out of sincerity and humility reading His word, and praying daily.

Not only did Jesus Christ (Yeshua Hamashiach) live a sinless life, but He also taught about the Kingdom of Heaven, showing us how to live and what it takes to enter His Kingdom. He demonstrated selflessness and service and brought the good news of salvation, a free gift from God (Yahweh), not of works lest any man should boast. We don't earn it through our own efforts.

Jesus Christ (Yeshua Hamashiach) became poor so that we may become rich. He showed selflessness and service, wanting everyone to come to Him as they are. He is the Light of the world, King of Kings, and Lord and Savior. He loved us enough to die for us and gets all the glory, honor, and praise. Words cannot describe how I feel knowing what He did that day on Calvary.

Purposes Jesus Christ (Yeshua Hamashiah) Came
Jesus Christ (Yeshua Hamashiach) came to this world for specific purposes:

Reconciliation: Jesus Christ (Yeshua Hamashiach) came to reconcile humanity with God (Yahweh), to proclaim the Kingdom of God (Yahweh), calling people to live according to the will of God (Yahweh).

Salvation and Redemption: Fulfilled God's (Yahweh's) plan of redemption, saving humanity from sin and death.

Forgiveness: Jesus Christ (Yeshua Hamashiach) offered humanity forgiveness and a new life through faith.

Relationship: With each one of us, if we receive Jesus Christ (Yeshua Hamashiach) and believe in the Gospel and what He did for us all.

To destroy the works of the Devil (Satan): Jesus Christ (Yeshua Hamashiach) also came to destroy the works of Satan.

Satan is the God of this world

1 John 3:8 [8] To this end the Son of God was revealed: that he might destroy the works of the devil, (Satan).

2 Corinthians 4:4 [4] In whom the god of this world hath blinded the minds of them which believe not, lest the light of the glorious gospel of Christ, who is the image of God, should shine unto them.

John 8:44 [44] Ye are of your father the devil, and the lusts of your father ye will do. He was a murderer from the beginning, and abode not in the truth, because there is no truth in him. When he speaketh a lie, he speaketh of his own: for he is a liar, and the father of lies.

When he speaketh a lie, he speaketh of his own: for he is a liar, and the father of it.

1 Peter 5:8 [8] Be sober, be vigilant; because your adversary the devil, as a roaring lion, walketh about, seeking whom he may devour.

Matthew 16:23 [23] But he turned, and said unto Peter, get thee behind me, Satan: thou art an offence unto me: for thou savourest not the things that be of God, but those that be of men.

1 Corinthians 7:5 [5] Defraud ye not one the other, except it be with consent for a time, that ye may give yourselves to fasting and prayer: and come together again, that Satan tempt you not for your incontinency.

Jesus Christ (Yeshua Hamashiach) demonstrated authority over Satan's kingdom and the powers of darkness of this world. Through Jesus Christ's (Yeshua Hamashiach) life, death, and resurrection, He achieved victory over spiritual oppression, demonic forces, and the works of the Devil (Satan). At Jesus Christ's (Yeshua Hamashiach) second coming, the ultimate defeat of evil will be realized, and He will judge the living and the dead and establish His eternal Kingdom.

Hebrews 2:14-15 [14] Forasmuch then as the children are partakers of flesh and blood, he also himself likewise took part of the same; that through death he might destroy him that had the power of death, that is, the devil; [15] And deliver them who through fear of death were all their lifetime subject to bondage.

John 12:31 [31]Now is the judgment of this world: now shall the prince of this world be cast out.

Revelation 20:10 [10]And the devil that deceived them was cast into the lake of fire and brimstone, where the beast and the false prophet are, and shall be tormented day and night for ever and ever.

Chapter 2
The 4 Gospels according to the Apostles

The Gospel of Jesus Christ (Yeshua Hamashiach) according to Paul, is found in the New Testament:

1 Corinthians 15: 1-4 [1]**Moreover, brethren, I declare unto you the gospel which I preached unto you, which also ye have received, and wherein ye stand;** [2]**By which also ye are saved, if ye keep in memory what I preached unto you, unless ye have believed in vain.** [3]**For I delivered unto you first of all that which I also received, how that Jesus Christ (Yeshua Hamashiach), died for our sins according to the scriptures;** [4]**And that he was buried, and that he rose again the third day. All according to the scriptures:**

The Gospel of Romans 3: 24-26 [24] written by Paul the Apostle

Romans 3: 24-26 [24] Being justified freely by his grace through the redemption that is in Yeshua: [25] Whom Yah "Our Heavenly Father" hath set forth to be a propitiation through faith in his blood, to declare his righteousness for the remission of sins that are past, through the forbearance of God (Yahweh); [26] To declare, I say, at this time his righteousness: that he might be just, and the justifier of him which believeth in Yeshua.

The Gospel of Romans 10: 9-10 written by Paul the Apostle

Romans 10:9-10 [9] If you confess with your mouth Jesus Christ (Yeshua Hamashiach) and believe in your heart that God (Yahweh) raised him from the dead, you will be saved. [10] For with the heart man believeth unto righteousness; and with the mouth confession is made unto salvation.

The Gospel of St John 3: 16-18 written by John the Apostle

St. John 3:16-18 [16] For God (Yahweh) so loved the world that he gave his only begotten Son, that whosoever believeth in him should not perish, but have everlasting life. [17] For God (Yahweh) sent not his Son into the world to condemn the world: but that the world through him might be saved. [18] He that believeth on him is not condemned: but he that believeth not is condemned already, because he hath not believed in the name of the only begotten Son of God.

Chapter 3
All Paths Do NOT Lead to God! (Yahweh) and the pastors who don't teach Biblical Truths.

The idea that all paths lead to God (Yahweh) is a common belief, but it is not supported by all religions. There are not many roads to God (Yahweh): only one. Christianity teaches that Jesus Christ (Yeshua Hamashiach) is the only way to God (Yahweh). In Christianity, God (Yahweh) seeks man and breaks into all paths. Other religions have different beliefs about creation, sin, heaven, hell, God (Yahweh), and salvation, and their truth claims conflict with each other. Therefore, it is not possible that all paths lead to God (Yahweh).

Jesus (Yeshua) did not say, "For God (Yahweh) so loved the world that He gave Muhammed, Confucius, Odin, John Shelby Spong, Zeus, or Sylvia Browne, that whoever believes in any or all of them shall have everlasting life."

God's, (Yahweh's) plan of salvation involves His "one and only Son." There is only one road to God (Yahweh).

Jesus Christ (Yeshua Hamashiach) came so that the world might be saved through Him. Apart from Him, there is no salvation, only judgment: "He who believes in Him is not judged; he who does not believe has been judged already, because he has not believed in the name of the only begotten Son of God (Yahweh). This is the judgment, that the Light has come into the world, and men loved the darkness rather than the Light, for their deeds were evil," by the Lord Jesus Christ (Yeshua Hamashiach's) own words.

There are not many roads to God (Yahweh): **"God (Yahweh) commands all people everywhere to repent." Acts 17:30** and trust in Jesus Christ (Yeshua Hamashiach), for **"salvation is found in no one else, for there is no other name under heaven given to mankind by which we must be saved." Acts 4:12.** There is no other road to God (Yahweh), so **"how shall we escape if we neglect so great a salvation?" Hebrews 2:3**

Scripture says that anyone who teaches another way of salvation is a false teacher in danger of damnation.

Knowing Jesus Christ (Yeshua Hamashiach) requires a heart willing to be molded and transformed by the Holy Spirit.

A stark reminder that religious activity or mighty works in Jesus Christ's (Yeshua Hamashiach) name are not indicators of genuine faith. It's not about the volume of religious or good deeds one does, but about the genuineness of our relationship with Jesus (Yeshua).

John 3:18-19 [18] By the Lord Jesus Christs' (Yeshua Hamashiach's) own words, anyone who does not believe in Him is already judged.

Acts 17:30 [30]and trust in Jesus Christ, for "salvation is found in no one else, for there is no other name under heaven given to mankind by which we must be saved."

Acts 4:12 [12] There is no other road to God, so "how shall we escape if we neglect so great a salvation?"

Hebrews 2:3 [3] How shall we escape, if we neglect so great salvation; which at the first began to be spoken

by the Lord, and was confirmed unto us by them that heard him;

1 Timothy 2:5 [5] For there is one God, and one mediator between God and men, the man Christ Jesus;

Galatians 1:6-9 [6] I marvel that ye are so soon removed from him that called you into the grace of Christ unto another gospel: [7] Which is not another; but there be some that trouble you, and would pervert the gospel of Christ. [8]But though we, or an angel from heaven, preach any other gospel unto you than that which we have preached unto you, let him be accursed. [9]As we said before, so say I now again, if any man preaches any other gospel unto you than that ye have received, let him be accursed. Those who proclaim, "All roads lead to God," are perverters of the gospel and deniers of "the faith that was once for delivered to the saints"

To pastors who do not teach 100% Biblical truths:

Matthew 15:9 [9]But in vain they do worship me, Teaching for doctrines the commandments of men.

Jeremiah 23:1 [1]Woe be unto the pastors that destroy and scatter the sheep of my pasture! Saith the LORD.

Does Jesus Christ (Yeshua Hamashiach) know you? Are you intimate with our Heavenly Father by reading the Bible to learn God's word, and praying daily, repenting of sins when we do? "Repent" means to turn around. Seeking a relationship with Jesus (Yeshua) is key. It's not about religion. Jesus (Yeshua) doesn't like all these religions anyway. When He comes back, He will set the record straight!

There is an exchange that takes place when you give your life to Jesus Christ (Yeshua Hamashiach), making Him Lord and Savior of your life. When you do, He expects you to give your life to Him, every part of that. We are to repent from any future sins when we do and depend on Him every day to provide and take care of us in every area of our lives. Without Jesus Christ (Yeshua Hamashiach), we are nothing. You have to have faith and believe in His promises, which are written throughout the scriptures. If you do not, you are going to hold onto some area in your life, not letting Jesus (Yeshua) take care of it, and that part of your life can become messy if it isn't given over to him to handle.

Chapter 4
Salvation, Receiving the Holy Spirit, Baptism (an outward expression of your faith), and the Scriptures Pertaining to them

Salvation, Holy Spirit, and Baptism

Salvation occurs when you believe in Jesus Christ (Yeshua Hamashiach) and have faith in the blood atonement of what He did on the cross for us. There's nothing you can do to earn salvation; it's a free gift that Jesus Christ (Yeshua Hamashiach) paid for. It is through faith in Jesus Christ (Yeshua Hamashiach) that believers receive this free gift. Salvation costs us even though it's free. What do I mean by that? Jesus Christ (Yeshua Hamashiach) paid for you, so He owns you. There is a commitment on your part once you receive salvation, to give your life over to Jesus (Yeshua). Surrender to God's (Yahweh's) will and purpose. Jesus Christ (Yeshua Hamashiach) wants everyone to come to Him as they are.

Jesus Christ (Yeshua Hamashiach) is the light of the world; He is the way, the truth, and the life. Our true King of Kings.

Salvation is a free gift from God (Yahweh); it is accompanied by the responsibility to live righteously and demonstrate faith through actions. The door into God's (Yahweh's) kingdom, the door of salvation, is a commitment and doesn't warrant dabbling in the Kingdom and dabbling in the world. When you choose to follow Jesus Christ (Yeshua Hamashiach) and not the world.

A quote from Pastor Enrique Pascal: "I came across an interview on YouTube of a preacher who preaches the Word of God (Yahweh)." He said, "Heaven is not for people who live, but people who die." Die to self, your ego, and your emotions, as hell is for those who choose to live it up; in other words, if you party and do your own thing, then why would you need God (Yahweh)? You would be your own God. True salvation is when you give Jesus Christ (Yeshua Hamashiach), who died for all, your life. Since He paid for your life, we need to give our lives to Him.

Holy Spirit: The moment you believe, receive, and make Jesus Christ (Yeshua Hamaschiach) Lord and Savior of your life, trusting in Him alone, He will give you the Holy Spirit to reside in you to teach you all things to come. This will enable you to be equipped in every area of your life. The Holy Spirit will comfort you, guide you, convict you, lead you, intercede for you, and give you revelation. Your body is a temple for the Holy Spirit to dwell in. The Holy Spirit will help you fix what needs to change. Be perfect (meaning be mature), as I am perfect, God (Yahweh) says. Don't be a child, meaning put away a sinful life.

The Holy Spirit gives gifts to each person individually as He wills. The gifts of the Holy Spirit are:

1. Word of wisdom

2. Word of knowledge

3. Gift of faith

4. Gift of healing

5. Working of miracles

6. Prophecy

7. Distinguishing between spirits

8. Speaking in tongues

9. Interpreting tongues

Some Bible Verses About the Holy Spirit

John 14:26 [26] **But the Comforter, which is the Holy Ghost, whom the Father will send in my name, he shall teach you all things, and bring all things to your remembrance, whatsoever I have said unto you.**

John 16:13 [13] **Howbeit when he, the Spirit of truth, is come, he will guide you into all truth: for he shall not speak of himself; but whatsoever he shall hear, that shall he speak: and he will shew you things to come.**

Galatians 5:22-23 [22] **But the fruit of the Spirit is love, joy, peace, longsuffering, gentleness, goodness, faith.**

1 Corinthians 2:10 [2] **But God hath revealed them unto us by his Spirit: for the Spirit searcheth all things, yea, the deep things of God.**

Acts 2:38 [38] Then Peter said unto them, Repent, and be baptized every one of you in the name of Jesus Christ for the remission of sins, and ye shall receive the gift of the Holy Ghost.

Acts 2:33 [33] Therefore being by the right hand of God exalted, and having received of the Father the promise of the Holy Ghost, he hath shed forth this, which ye now see and hear.

John 14:15-17 [15] If ye love me, keep my commandments.

Galatians 1:12 [12] For I neither received it of man, neither was I taught it, but by the revelation of Jesus Christ.

Proverbs 2:1-5 [1] My son, if thou wilt receive my words, and hide my commandments with thee;

2 Timothy 1:7 [7] For God hath not given us the spirit of fear; but of power, and of love, and of a sound mind.

1 Corinthians 6:19 [6] **What? know ye not that your body is the temple of the Holy Ghost which is in you, which ye have of God, and ye are not your own?**

John 15:15 [15] **Henceforth I call you not servants; for the servant knoweth not what his lord doeth: but I have called you friends; for all things that I have heard of my Father I have made known unto you.**

The call to Baptism

It is a call to decide whether one is truly ready to declare that Jesus Christ (Yeshua Hamashiach) is the Lord and to submit to the Spirit's sanctifying work, which begins with a clean slate—a fresh start. Baptism is what you spiritually do. It is an outward expression of your faith.

Belief in Jesus Christ (Yeshua Hamashiach) as the Messiah is essential for salvation, as stated in:

Mark 16:16 [16]**"Whoever believes and is baptized will be saved."**

Baptism is an outward sign of faith and commitment, symbolizing the washing away of sins and the receiving of the Holy Spirit

Acts 2:38 [38] "Repent and be baptized, every one of you, in the name of Jesus Christ for the forgiveness of your sins."

When we believe in the finished work of Jesus Christ (Yeshua Hamashiach) and accept His sacrificial blood atonement, the moment we make Him our personal Lord and Savior, we are new creatures in Jesus Christ (Yeshua Hamashiach) and are saved. Worshipping Jesus Christ (Yeshua Hamashiach) every day in spirit and in truth, being obedient to reading His word, and walking not only in love but also choosing the narrow path is what He requires of us. Though we have free will, there are blessings that Jesus (Yeshua) bestows on those who choose to pick up their cross daily and follow Him instead of the world. Choosing to walk the way Jesus Christ (Yeshua Hamashiach) would have us walk is a daily commitment. When we give Jesus Christ (Yeshua Hamashiach) our lives, picking up our own cross and renewing our minds daily while walking in faith is a requirement.

Grace is something we didn't earn and we don't deserve. Our Heavenly Father (Yahweh) gave His only begotten son that whosoever believes in Him will not perish but have eternal life. When we admit we are sinners in need of Jesus Christ (Yeshua Hamashiach), the moment we make Him our personal Lord and Savior and put our faith and trust in Jesus Christs' (Yeshua Hamashiach's) blood, we surrender all of our life to Him as He died for us. Then we are saved and are justified by the blood of Jesus Christ (Yeshua Hamashiach).

When you give your life to Jesus Christ (Yeshua Hamashiach) you are giving Him your old life. When you say yes and give your life to Jesus Christ (Yeshua Hamashiach), He can live in and through you. You surrender your life and accept His will for every area of your life. If you repent for any sins (go in another direction) and ask the Holy Spirit to help you fix what needs to change. Be perfect (meaning be mature) as I am perfect, God (Yahweh) says: "Don't be a child," meaning put away a sinful life.

When you put your faith and trust in the finished work of Jesus Christ (Yeshua Hamashiach), He will require all of your life. The good days and bad days. Every day we are to die to self; we are not to take it upon ourselves and do everything ourselves. Apart from Him, as He says, you can do nothing. Jesus Christ (Yeshua Hamashiach) works in and through us with the help and guidance of the Holy Spirit. Jesus Christ (Yeshua Hamashiach) gives to each and every one of us to dwell within us when we make Him Lord and Savior of our lives. When we seek Him every day. When we worship Him in spirit and in truth, when we say yes to Jesus Christ (Yeshua Hamashiach), to His will for our lives, He blesses us, and we become new creatures in and through Him.

2 Corinthians 5:17 [17] Therefore if any man be in Christ, he is a new creature: old things are passed away; behold, all things are become new.

1 John 5:11-13 [11]And this is the record, that God hath given to us eternal life, and this life is in his Son. [12] He that hath the Son hath life; and he that hath not the Son of God hath not life. [13]These things have I written unto you that believeth on the name of the Son

of God: that ye may know that ye have eternal life, and that ye may believe on the name of the Son of God.

John 15:5 [5] I am the vine: you are the branches. If you remain in me and I in you, you will bear much fruit, apart from me you can do nothing.

Chapter 5
Repentance, Grace, Mercy & a Prayer

The Bible never teaches to repent of your sins to be saved. That is not what it says. The Bible says to trust in Jesus Christ's (Yeshua Hamashich's) sacrificial blood atonement and what He did on the cross for ALL, make Him Lord and Savior of your life, and trust in Him alone for Him to direct your path daily, and then you're saved. When we receive Jesus Christ (Yeshua Hamashiach) as Lord and Savior, it is by grace that we are saved and not of good works. Doing good deeds for others is something we, as believers, should do, but it's by grace we are saved and not of works.

Repentance involves turning away from sin and acknowledging one's need for forgiveness. Jesus Christ (Yeshua Hamashiach) will meet you wherever you are, exactly how you are. There is no sin so great that He won't forgive if you are genuine in asking Him for forgiveness. All who truly repent of their sins and, by turning away from them in full surrender by faith when they accept Jesus Christ (Yeshua Hamashiach) as their personal Lord and Savior, will have their sins forgiven. It's by an act of divine grace, and they will be reborn in the spirit as they walk according to His will for you.

Romans 3:23 ²³ For all have sinned and come short of the glory of God.

Lamentations 3:22 ²² It is of the Lord's mercies that we are not consumed, because his compassions fail not. ²³They are new every morning: great is thy faithfulness.

It is through God's (Yahweh's) grace and mercy that we ask Him in the mighty name of Jesus Christ (Yeshua Hamashiach) to forgive us in true repentance and sincerity. You can go to a quiet place even in your home and cry out to God (Yahweh); you don't need a church, a pastor, or a priest to do this. Finding a church that teaches scriptures from the Bible and a pastor that teaches the word of God (Yahweh), the scriptures, psalms, and prayers, and how to live is beneficial to your walk with

Jesus Christ (Yeshua Hamashiach). Jesus Christ (Yeshua Hamashiach) says that if you abide in His words and His words abide in you, learning scriptures leads to answered prayers. Trust in Him alone, and He will direct your path.

John 15:7 [7] If ye abide in me, and my words abide in you, ye shall ask what ye will, and it shall be done unto you.

Religious activity or mighty works in Jesus Christ's (Yeshua Hamashiach) name are not indicators of genuine faith. It is not about the volume of religious or good deeds one does, but about the genuineness of our relationship with Jesus Christ (Yeshua Hamashiach).

One way to hear from Him is through prayer and reading God's (Yahweh's) word. When you pray and ask God (Yahweh) to speak to you through His word, ask the Holy Spirit for guidance on how to approach the word. Ask Him to open your eyes and heart to hear from Him. Here is a sample prayer:

Dear Lord,

Thank You for Your Word and Your Will.

Thank You for allowing me to learn more about You.

Please help me hear the small voice of the Holy Spirit.

Please help me understand the message that You, O Lord, have for me, and help me put it into practice in my life.

Please give me wisdom to discern, a humble heart to accept, and courage to do Your will.

In the mighty name and blood of Jesus Christ (Yeshua Hamashiach), I pray. Amen.

When you meditate on the Word of God (Yahweh), you feed your mind by reading and getting God's (Yahweh's) word down in your soul. When we learn Scripture and speak it out of our mouths in confession to the promises of God (Yahweh), or decreeing and declaring what He says, it is a spiritual principle of calling things that are not as though they were. When words are spoken in faith that comes by hearing the Word of God (Yahweh), if it's in the will of God (Yahweh), by calling for what you desire in faith and what doesn't exist, you call until it manifests in God's (Yahweh's) time. If it doesn't manifest, that means He has something better for you.

When you speak of the end results, it's a method of calling things that are not, and by practicing it, you are to develop in it.

Romans 4:17 [17] **(As it is written, I have made thee a father of many nations), before him whom he believed, even God, who quickeneth the dead, and calleth those things which be not as though they were.**

Chapter 6
The Blood of Jesus Christ (Yeshua Hamashiach)

Why Plead the Blood of Jesus Christ (Yeshua Hamashiach)?

Jesus Christ (Yeshua Hamashiach) is the Way, the Truth, and the Life. Life is in the Blood. Trust in the blood of Jesus Christ (Yeshua Hamashiach) and what He did for us on the cross. No man comes to the Father except through Him. When you say yes to Jesus Christ (Yeshua Hamashiach), He'll take away everything that stands in the way of you being in a relationship with Him. Then He can live in and through you when you surrender your life, when you accept His will for you in every area of your life

When we plead the blood of Jesus Christ (Yeshua Hamashiach) over our lives, we are calling upon the divine power that was established through Jesus Christ (Yeshua Hamashiach's) sacrifice, recognizing His blood brings healing, protection, deliverance, and restoration.

This practice is rooted in Biblical teachings, particularly in:

Revelation 12:11 [11]which states, **"And they overcame him by the blood of the Lamb and by the word of their testimony."** Believers have victory through that verse, emphasizing the blood of Jesus Christ (Yeshua Hamashiach) over spiritual adversaries. You are putting your confidence in an oath that is covenant-sworn by Almighty God (Yahweh).

By pleading Jesus Christ (Yeshua Hamashiach's) blood, you are taking the power and authority granted to you by God (Yahweh) Himself and putting it to work in your life, just as He intended. By pleading the blood of Jesus Christ (Yeshua Hamashiach), you are speaking out in faith with confidence and boldness so that the devil doesn't get a foothold in your life. Personally, I plead the Blood of Jesus Christ (Yeshua Hamashiach) over every part of my life on a daily basis: over my body, mind, spirit, soul, my home, etc.

An example of pleading the blood: You can plead the blood over yourself or any situation:

Our Heavenly Father, (Yahweh), "I plead the blood of Jesus Christ (Yeshua Hamashiach) over me" or over this vehicle and all who are in it. "That we will go and come back safely."

Some scriptures that speak on the Blood of Jesus Christ (Yeshua Hamashiach):

1 John 1:7 [7]But if we walk in the light, as he is in the light, we have fellowship one with another, and the blood of Jesus Christ his Son cleanseth us from all sin.

Hebrews 9:22 [22]And almost all things are by the law purged with blood; and without shedding of blood is no remission.

Hebrews 9:14 [14] How much more shall the blood of Christ, who through the eternal Spirit offered himself without spot to God, purge your conscience from dead works to serve the living God?

Romans 5:9 [9] Much more then, being now justified by his blood, we shall be saved from wrath through him.

1 John 1:7-9 [7] But if we walk in the light, as he is in the light, we have fellowship one with another, and the blood of Jesus Christ his Son cleanseth us from all sin.

Revelation 12:11 [11] And they overcame him by the blood of the Lamb, and by the word of their testimony; and they loved not their lives unto the death.

Acts 20:28 [28] Take heed therefore unto yourselves, and to all the flock, over the which the Holy Ghost hath made you overseers, to feed the church of God, which he hath purchased with his own blood.

Revelation 1:5 [5] And from Jesus Christ, who is the faithful witness, and the first begotten of the dead, and the prince of the kings of the earth. Unto him that loved us, and washed us from our sins in his own blood,

Hebrews10:19 [19]Having therefore, brethren, boldness to enter into the holiest by the blood of Jesus,

Romans 3: 24-25 [24]Being justified freely by his grace through the redemption that is in Christ Jesus:

Ephesians 1:7 [7] In whom we have redemption through his blood, the forgiveness of sins, according to the riches of his grace;

1 Peter 1:18-19 [19] Forasmuch as ye know that ye were not redeemed with corruptible things, as silver and gold, from your vain conversation received by tradition from your fathers;

Revelation 7:14 [14] And I said unto him, Sir, thou knowest. And he said to me, these are they which came out of great tribulation, and have washed their robes, and made them white in the blood of the Lamb.

John 6: 50-71 [50] This is the bread which cometh down from heaven, that a man may eat thereof, and not die...

Hebrews 13:12 [12] Wherefore Jesus also, that he might sanctify the people with his own blood, suffered without the gate.

Leviticus 17:11 [11] For the life of the flesh is in the blood: and I have given it to you upon the altar to make an atonement for your souls: for it is the blood that maketh an atonement for the soul.

1 Corinthians 11:24-30 [24] And when he had given thanks, he brake it, and said, Take, eat: this is my body, which is broken for you: this do in remembrance of me...

John 6:55-59 [55] For my flesh is meat indeed, and my blood is drink indeed...

Colossians 1:20 [20] And, having made peace through the blood of his cross, by him to reconcile all things unto himself; by him, I say, whether they be things in earth, or things in heaven.

Revelation 5:9 [9] And they sung a new song, saying, Thou art worthy to take the book, and to open the seals thereof: for thou wast slain, and hast redeemed us to God by thy blood out of every kindred, and tongue, and people, and nation;

Hebrews 10: 6-9 [6] In burnt offerings and sacrifices for sin thou hast had no pleasure...

Chapter 7
The difference between the Old and New Testament Covenants

The Old and New Testament Covenant

The book of Hebrews talks about the differences between the Old and New Testaments. Here are a few verses talking about this.

Hebrews 10: 8-13 **[8]Above when he said, Sacrifice and offering and burnt offerings and offering for sin thou wouldest not, neither hadst pleasure therein: which are offered by the law: [9] Then said he, Lo, I come to do thy will, O God. He taketh away the first, that he may establish the second. [10] By the which will we are sanctified through the offering of the body of Jesus Christ (Yeshua Hamashiach) once for all. [11] And every priest standeth daily ministering and offering oftentimes the same sacrifices, which can never take away sins: [12] But this man, after he had offered one**

sacrifice for sins forever, sat down on the right hand of God (Yahweh): [13] From henceforth expecting till his enemies be made his footstool.

The Old Covenant

The Old Covenant was the working arrangement God (Yahweh) established with Israel, found in the Old Testament, and consists of 39 documents that give us details of the Old Covenant, which was rooted in the Mosaic Law and includes physical promises, rituals, and sacrifices for atonement, laying the groundwork for understanding sin and the need for atonement. God (Yahweh) didn't have this relationship with any other group of people as He had with Israel. He established a sacrificial system allowing them to be temporarily cleansed of their sins by these sacrifices. They were repeated over and over by an ordained priest, as the people couldn't come directly to God (Yahweh). The nation came under the judgment of God (Yahweh) as they were unfaithful. The people repeatedly broke the law, violating the covenant. The sacrifices for the blood of bulls and goats were annual reminders of their sins, yet these priests, who were performing these religious duties by offering the same sacrifices again and again, could not take away sins. Jesus Christ (Yeshua Hamashiach) demonstrated His ultimate act of grace and mercy so we can come to Him freely, as He made a new covenant with us, which is better than the Old Covenant.

The New Covenant

The new covenant Jesus Christ (Yeshua Hamashiach) made with us is found in the New Testament part of the Bible, fulfilled by Jesus Christ (Yeshua Hamashiach). Jesus Christ (Yeshua Hamashiach) offers us a new way of relating to God (Yahweh) by emphasizing grace through faith and spiritual forgiveness, fulfilling God's (Yahweh's) promises of salvation. The transition from the law to grace is found in the New Testament, consisting of 27 documents detailing the sacrifice of Jesus Christ (Yeshua Hamashiach) under the New Covenant He made with us. A means by which sins can be forgiven once and for all.

Religious Leaders, Councils, and the Books of the Bible

There were various religious leaders and councils over the centuries who determined which books were included in the Bible and excluded. The excluded books were viewed as lacking the inspiration and necessary authority to be considered part of canonical Scripture. These books were rejected based on criteria established by the early church leaders. Many people, including myself, believe that they removed these books to keep us ignorant of the truth.

The Catholic Bible contains 73 books, while the Protestant versions have 66, and Eastern Orthodox churches include more texts. The Ethiopian Orthodox Church includes 81 books in its biblical canon. Eastern Orthodox Churches have more additional books than the Catholic edition.

The Catholic authorities recognize the Old Testament books in the Bible called the Apocrypha, found in the Greek Septuagint and Latin Vulgate, yet absent from the Hebrew Bible, and continue to include deuterocanonical books in their teaching and worship, while Protestant churches teach and worship from the 66-book canon. The last 14 books containing the Apocrypha that makes up the Old Testament in the Catholic Bible is as follows: 1 Esdras, 2 Esdras, Tobit, Judith, the rest of Esther, The Wisdom of Solomon, Ecclesiasticus, Baruch with the epistle Jeremiah, The Songs of the 3 Holy Children, The History of Susana, Bel and the Dragon, The Prayer of Manasseh, 1 Maccabees, and 2 Maccabees'.

In 1684, the Vatican removed all 14 books of the Bible except the 1611 edition: the first edition translated into English. In that edition, Jesus' name is spelled IESUS and pronounced Yahashua or Ishuyah. The letter J wasn't in usage until the early 1400's to early 1500's B.C., yet we still call our savior Jesus.

In the 16th century, the Protestant Reformation movement led by Martin Luther had made biblical decisions across denominations to exclude the Apocrypha from their Bible versions. He favored the Masoretic Text, which is a Hebrew version of the Old Testament. That didn't include the Septuagint, the Greek version of the Old Testament used by early Christians. The Protestant churches worldwide adopted the decisions made by Martin Luther on what to include in the deuterocanonical books we have today.

In Martin Luther's 1534 German Bible translation, he labeled these books as "Apocrypha," and the early Protestant Bibles didn't remove the Apocrypha entirely but kept them as separate sections. The Protestant publishers excluded the books from the Apocrypha over time throughout the mid-17th century, yet the 1611 version of the King James Bible, which was translated from Latin to English, contains 80 books, including the Apocrypha.

Chapter 8
Amillennialism, Denominations, and Replacement Theology

Amillennialism is a common belief among Protestant denominations such as Lutheran, Reformed, Anglican, and Methodist, and many Jews. Amillennialists believe the millennium is simultaneous with this present age. They also believed Satan was already bound and that Revelation 20 had occurred when that actually occurs at the beginning of the millennium, and that hasn't happened yet!

Amillennialism can sometimes be associated with idealism. They both teach that the prophecies in the book of Revelation are nothing more than symbolic. For those who believe this, they have another thing coming! Some do believe in a literal fulfillment of prophecies; they can't agree on when these prophecies will be fulfilled.

FACT: The millennium isn't simultaneously happening with this present age, and the binding of Satan has not already occurred! The Millennium has not happened yet! Jesus Christ (Yeshua Hamashiach) did not come back yet. He did not rapture the believers (called saints), including Jew and Gentile, or have a wedding feast with His bride! Nor did he come back with the Saints (believers, including Jews and Gentiles) and angels on white horses to fight the Devil (Satan) in the Battle of Armageddon. That didn't take place yet! The final time Jesus Christ (Yeshua Hamashiach) comes, He will physically reign on a New Earth with New Jerusalem coming down from the New Heaven, which has a wall with twelve gates and at the gates twelve angels, a golden reed that measures the city that lies foursquare, and the length, breadth, and height of it are equal. Our Heavenly Father, God (Yahweh), has specific dimensions for the New Jerusalem City that believers will eternally dwell in, just like He had specific dimensions for the Ark Noah built.

Also, some Lutherans, Catholics, Methodists and other denominations, and churches teach that Jesus Christ's (Yeshua Hamashiach's) second coming already happened and that the 1000 years of peace are taking place now.

Some churches teach this, and it isn't true! That would mean:

Zechariah 14: 16-17 And it shall come to pass, that every one that is left of all the nations which came against Jerusalem shall even go up from year to year to worship the King, the LORD of hosts (that will be Jesus crowned King!) and to keep the feasts of tabernacles. [17] And it shall be, that whoso will not come up of all the families of the earth unto Jerusalem to worship the King, the LORD of hosts, even upon them shall be no rain.

There aren't ANY families living on the earth that from year to year go to the New Jerusalem to worship Jesus Christ (Yeshua Hamashiach), our Heavenly King, in person as of yet. When He physically reigns here, yes, we will be required to do so! To the people who believe in Amillennialism: That didn't happen yet!

Zechariah 14: 1-3 [1] Behold, the day of the LORD cometh, and thy spoil shall be divided in the midst of thee. [2] For I will gather all nations against Jerusalem to battle, and the city shall be taken, and the houses

rifled, and the women ravished: and half of the city shall go forth into captivity, and the residue of the people shall not be cut off from the city. [3] Then shall the Lord go forth, and fight against those nations, as when he fought in the day of battle.

Replacement Theology

Replacement theology teaches that the church has replaced Israel in God's (Yahweh's) plan. The attitude of some Christians is that the Jews are not as good as the Christians. When the church believes that in the new covenant, they receive all the promises of God (Yahweh), and the Jews are locked out of those promises, and that God (Yahweh) has a different plan for them during the 7 years of Tribulation and millennial reign, that is Replacement Theology. God (Yahweh) HATES Replacement Theology! God's (Yahweh's) plan is for Israel to preach the good news of the Messiah to all nations.

Covenant Theology emphasizes unity of God's (Yahweh's) people throughout history and doesn't teach that the church replaced Israel. The church and Israel are distinct and not to be used interchangeably.

Romans 11:16 [16] **The Apostle Paul wrote if the first piece of dough is holy the lump is also and if the root is holy the branches are too.**

There was a small percentage of Jews who came to believe in Israel. They kicked off the church 2000 years ago, and the Nation of Israel is also Holy because of Abraham, Isaac, and Jacob. Jacob is the seed from which all 12 tribes were born.

Chapter 9
Our Heavenly Father (Yahweh) wants no one to perish!

Confessing, believing in the blood atonement, trusting, and making Jesus Christ (Yeshua Hamashiach) the Lord and Savior of your life.

2 Peter 3: 9 [9] The Lord is not slack concerning his promise, as some men count slackness: but is longsuffering to us-ward. Not willing that any should perish, but that all should come to repentance.

GOD LOVES YOU

SIN SEPARATES PEOPLE FROM GOD

JESUS DIED FOR YOUR SINS

YOU CAN RECEIVE JESUS NOW

AND KNOW GOD'S LOVE.

"If you confess with your mouth and make Jesus Christ (Yeshua Hamashiach) your Lord and Savior, believe in your heart that God (Yahweh) raised Jesus Christ (Yeshua Hamashiach) from the dead, if you put your faith in his blood atonement, when you make Jesus Christ (Yeshua Hamashiach) Lord and Savior of your life, picking up your cross, following him daily, worshipping him in Spirit and in truth you shall be saved."

A sample prayer you could pray: Heavenly Father, in Jesus' (Yeshua's) name:

I repent of my sins and open my heart to let Jesus (Yeshua) come inside of me. Jesus (Yeshua), you are my Lord and Savior. I believe you died for my sins and you were raised from the dead. Fill me with your Holy Spirit. "Father, God (Yahweh), I recognize that I have not lived my life for You up until now. I have been living for myself, and that is wrong. I need You in my life; I want You in my life. I acknowledge the completed work of Your Son Jesus Christ (Yeshua Hamashiach) in giving His life for me on the cross at Calvary. I have faith in His blood atonement, and I long to receive the forgiveness you have made freely available to me through this sacrifice. Come into my life now, Lord. Take up residence in my heart and be my King, my Lord, and my Savior. From this day forward, I will no longer be controlled by sin or the desire to please myself, but I will follow You all the days of my life. Those days are in Your hands. I ask this in Jesus' (Yeshua's) precious and holy name. Amen."

Chapter 10
Over 2000+ prophecies coming to pass, and the Book of Revelations

As of the publication of this book in the year 2026:

Over 2000+ Bible prophecies have already come to pass.

We are living out specific Books of the Bible, one being the Book of Revelation.

The Book of Revelation generally outlines the order of events and themes as follows:

In Chronological Order:

1. **Introduction and Vision:** John receives a revelation from God (Yahweh) while on the island of Patmos. **(Revelation 1:1-3)**

2. **Letters to the Seven Churches:** Jesus addresses 7 churches in Asia Minor, providing commendations and warnings. **(Revelation 2-3)**

3. **Heavenly Vision:** John sees a vision of God's throne and the worship in heaven. **(Revelation 4)**

4. **The Seven Seals:** The Lamb opens the seven seals of a scroll, leading to various events, including the Four Horsemen of the Apocalypse. **(Revelation 5-6)**

5. **The Seven Trumpets:** Seven angels sound trumpets, and bring about plagues and disasters on the earth. **(Revelation 8-11)**

6. **The Two Witnesses:** Two prophets prophesy in Jerusalem and eventually are killed. **(Revelation 11:3-14)**

7. **The Woman and the Dragon:** A symbolic representation of the struggle between good and evil. **(Revelation 12)**

8. **The Beasts and the Mark of the Beast:** The rise of the beast and the implementation of the mark. **(Revelation 13)**

The Seven Bowls of Wrath: Seven angels pour out God's wrath on the earth. **(Revelation 15-16)**

10. The Fall of Babylon: The judgment and destruction of Babylon, symbolizing the corrupt world system. **(Revelation 17-18)**

11. The Marriage Supper of the Lamb: The celebration of the union between Jesus Christ and His bride. **(Revelation 19:6-10)**

12. The Final Battle: The battle of Armageddon, where Christ defeats the beast and false prophet. **(Revelation 19:11-21)**

13. The Millennium: Christ reigns for a thousand years, and Satan is bound. **(Revelation 20:1-6)**

14. The Final Judgment: The dead are judged according to their deeds. **(Revelation 20:11-15)**

15. New Heaven and New Earth: The establishment of anew heaven and earth, where God dwells with His people. **(Revelation 21-22)**

Every day Bible prophecies have been coming to pass at an alarming rate as we are on the cusp of when Jesus

Christ (Yeshua Hamashiach) makes His glorious appearance, coming in the clouds to rapture His sheep (called the Saints). They are followers of Jesus Christ (Yeshua Hamashiach) who prepare themselves, look for Jesus' (Yeshua's) his coming, and pray every day to be found worthy to be a part of what is called a "Harpazo", or Rapture.

A rapture is a "snatching away," a rapid transportation to heaven without dying, and that is the basic meaning given to it by some religious people—that they will be instantly taken along to heaven in their fleshly bodies.

In the Gospel of Mark, Jesus' (Yeshua's) words are quoted at **Mark 13:24-27:**

24"But in those days, after that tribulation, the sun shall be darkened, and the moon shall not give her light. 25And the stars of heaven shall fall, and the powers that are in heaven shall be shaken. 26And then shall they see the Son of man coming in the clouds with great power and glory. 27And then shall he send his angels, and shall gather together his elect from the four winds, from the uttermost part of the earth to the uttermost part of heaven.

Chapter 11
What year was the Rapture taught?

How many Raptures are in the Bible?

What is the Final Judgment of the Nations?

The Rapture was taught back in the 1600s.

A rapture is the transportation of a living person to heaven without dying. It's called a "catching away" or (Harpazo). The following names, are people who taught the Rapture back in the 1600s. Morgan Edwards (1722-1795), Ephraem the Syrian (AD c.303-373), Irenaeus, Against Heresies, The Ante-Nicene Fathers, Lucian (died 312), Theodore (AD 350-428), Chrysostom (AD 354-407), Theodore (AD 386-458), & Diodorus of Tarsus all believed in the rapture. Early Christians, after the Apostles, taught this, including Justin Martyr, Irenaeus, Tertullian & Methodius. The Apostles believed in the imminent return of Christ, the Rapture of the Saints saved from the tribulation, a literal Antichrist, and the return of Christ.

Cyprian (AD 200-258)—Treatises of Cyprian, Victorinus (240-303), Thomas Vincent (1634-1678), Joseph Mede (1586-1639) Jeremiah Burroughs (1600-1646) Nathaniel Homes (1599-1678), William Aspinwall (1605-1662), John Browne (1582-1659), William Hook (1600-1677).

There are scriptures referring to God (Yahweh) snatching people away. There were 3 that happened from the beginning of time until Jesus. The last 4 will take place around the time of the 7-year Tribulation.

There is a total of 7 Raptures in the Biblical Scriptures, which are as follows:

1. Enoch, in ancient times before the flood he was the first man to be raptured. He just disappeared and didn't die. **(Genesis 5:21-24) (Hebrews 11:5)**

2. Elijah, in a whirlwind he was sucked up into a Chariot and horses of fire like lightening. During the Tribulation he will return again and will die and resurrect and be raptured again. **(2 Kings 2:11) (Revelation 11)**

3. Jesus Christs' (Yeshua Hamashiachs') Ascension, at age 33, The Jews who were his own people demanded the Romans murder him and he was buried in a tomb guarded by 4 soldiers. Jesus Christ (Yeshua Hamashiach) rose from the dead three days and three nights later and broke out of the tomb to show everyone he was alive and never died again. 10 days before the feast of Pentecost, Jesus, was raptured, ascended to heaven in His resurrected body as his apostles watched him ascend. **(Acts 1:9-11)**

Jesus Christ (Yeshua Hamashiach) took the Old Testament believers with Him. You can find that in the book of Matthew. **(Matthew 27: 50-53)**

4. Church Age Saints believers who follow Jesus Christ (Yeshua Hamashiach) who are alive will be "caught up" in the air, in the clouds to meet him, we will be changed in the twinkling of an eye. Our resurrected bodies will be made perfect. **(1 Thessalonians 4: 13-18)**

5. The Two Witnesses, Moses and Elijah will be the only men preaching for 42 months during the Tribulation and then be killed. The entire world will see their bodies lying in the streets of Jerusalem. God will say "Come up hither!" and they too will rise. **(Revelation 11:3-12)**

6. Tribulation Believers are believers who remain faithful to their faith during the Great Tribulation, which will be at a time of immense hardship and divine judgement.

7. The Battle of Armageddon, the final wrath and judgement of all people all over the world to face God Yahweh and Jesus Christ Yeshua Hamashiach and Jesus will return as King! **(Revelation 14: 17-20)**

Revelation 1:10 [10] I was in the Spirit on the Lord's Day, and heard behind me a great voice, as of a trumpet.

Revelation 4:1 [1] "After this I looked, and, behold, a door was opened in heaven: and the first voice which I heard was as it were of a trumpet talking with me: which said, come up hither, and I will shew thee things which must be hereafter."

There are believers who believe we shouldn't take the mark of the beast when given and have to endure to the end of the Tribulation in order to be saved and raptured. They are ignoring the previous raptures, and Scripture tells us we are not appointed to wrath.

1 Thessalonians 5:9 [9] For God hath not appointed us to wrath, but to obtain salvation by our Lord Jesus Christ (Yeshua Hamashiach).

Hebrews 9:28 [28] So Christ, having been offered one to bear the sins of many: and unto them that look for him shall he appear a second time, not to deal with sin but to save those who are eagerly waiting for him.

Revelation 14: 17-20 [17] After the rapture (the catching away of Tribulation Believers) and marriage of the Lamb (Jesus Christ Yeshua Hamashiach) and supper of the Lamb, (The Feast) The raptured Saints, the armies of Heaven follow Jesus on white horses to the battle of Armageddon where they battle the demons and Satan that takes place at the end of the Tribulation. When all this takes place it's the beginning of Jacob's Trouble.

There are 2 different shofar and trumpet blasts. "The last trump" is different than the seventh trumpet judgement in the book of Revelation. During the last trump, that will be the last time Christians hear from Jesus Christ (Yeshua Hamashiach).

The Final Judgement of the Nations

Zephania 3:8-9 **⁹ Therefore wait ye upon me, saith the LORD, until the day that I rise up to the prey: for my determination is to gather the nations, that I may assemble the kingdoms, to and gather the nations and assemble the kingdoms to pour upon them mine indignation, even all my fierce anger: for all the earth shall be devoured with the fire of my jealousy. ⁹ For then will I turn to the people a pure language, that they may all call upon the name of the LORD, to serve him with one consent.**

The damned from all over the world will be gathered in the Valley of Megiddo and face wrath from Our Heavenly Father (Yahweh) when Jesus Christ (Yeshua Hamashiach) returns to this world as King.

Chapter 12
The signs everywhere, The Beast System,
And Prophecy found in the Dead Sea Scrolls
Along with a Brilliant Question to Consider
Signs are everywhere, intensifying as our earth goes through birth pains.

2020 was a pivotal time for most people to wake up to the times we are living in. We are living in the End Days prophecy. My hope is that everyone gets on board before it's too late! Trust in the Gospel and what Jesus Christ ((Yeshua Hamashiach) did on that cross in Calvary. Make Him Lord and Savior of your life and trust in Him alone.

We see the signs everywhere: Hurricanes, Tornadoes, Floods, and Volcano eruptions are intensifying as our earth is going through birth pains as described in the Bible, and it's Global. We are seeing the rise of Freedom of Speech being stripped away; they are banning parts of the Bible in Canada because they deem it hate speech.

The Beast System is slowly being implemented around the world

A.I. is taking over jobs. There's no more regulation on AI, and they are implementing digital IDs throughout the world in order to work, etc. When all is said and done globally, we will have a Central Bank Digital Currency, a QR code that tracks your every move. This information is out there and will apply to everyone, whether you're Republican or Democrat, no matter the party. What's taking place is all biblical and was prophesied long ago. As a tyrannical New World Order government will form under the Antichrist (Beast) of Revelation for 7 years, the worst time in history.

In the book of Revelation 13, it describes a time when no man can buy or sell without a mark on his right hand or forehead. There will be an Antichrist, what the Bible calls the Beast, who will take control of the Beast system and sit in the rebuilt 3rd Temple, declaring himself God and wanting to be worshipped. Jesus (Yeshua) will come back for His own and end this tyranny and start his reign. We need to confess any sins daily to get right with Him. Believe me, you don't want to be here and get left behind when this period of time comes, and it'll be here sooner than you think!

A prophecy found in the Dead Sea Scrolls

In Christian eschatology, the Great Tribulation is a period mentioned by Jesus Christ (Yeshua Hamashiach) in the Olivet Discourse as a sign that would occur in the times of the end. At Revelation 7:14, "the Great Tribulation" will be the second half of the Tribulation period. The prophecy told is that the Jubilee will begin in a year of Jubilee. About this I'm not completely sure.

Isaiah 61: 1-2 [1] The Spirit of the Lord God is upon me, because the Lord hath anointed me to preach good tidings unto the meek: he hath sent me to bind up the brokenhearted, to proclaim liberty to the captives, and the opening of the prison to them that are bound. [2] To

proclaim the acceptable year of the Lord, and the day of vengeance of our God: to comfort all that mourn.

Isaiah 63: 1-4 [1] Who is that cometh from Edom, with dyed garment from Bozrah? This that is glorious in his apparel, traveling in the greatness of his strength? I that speak in righteousness, mighty to save. [2] Wherefore art red in thine apparel, and thy garments like him that treadeth in the wine fat? [3] I have trodden the winepress alone: and of the people there was none with me: for I will tread them in mine anger, and trample them in my fury: and their blood shall be sprinkled upon my garments, and I will stain all my raiment. [4] For the day of vengeance is in mine heart, and the year of my redeemed is come.

I believe the year of my Redeemed that Jesus (Yeshua) talks about in his word might be in a Jubilee year, though I'm not completely sure. I have my thoughts on who the Beast of Revelation 13 is, as he seems to fit the description of him found in the Book of Isaiah 63: 1-5, the Book of Daniel, the 11th chapter, and the Book of Revelation 13. In the book of Daniel, the Beast of Revelation 13 describes a man who will come in peaceably and be strong with a small people. It also describes the person's role and/or title He will have at that time.

A Brilliant Question to Consider

If a removal of the church (believers, including both Jew and Gentile) is false, why has the Devil (Satan) and his demons spent so much time and energy convincing the occult world to write about an explanation for the removal of millions and billions of people? The Devil (Satan) knows the truth; he knows the Bible. He knows the plan of the removal of the church, Jesus' (Yeshua's) sheep, and believers (both Jew and Gentile). If it isn't true, why is the Devil (Satan) wasting so much time laying down a narrative to explain it after it happens? - Braman House

The topic of UFOs and aliens (Aliens are fallen Angels). They walk this earth, have been in the news more now than ever, and most people have heard that they will be the reason for the disappearance of all those people. However, it will not be anything else other than Jesus Christ (Yeshua Hamashiach) removing believers in Him who make themselves ready for his return.

There are scriptures in the Bible that support a Rapture of a bride that Jesus (Yeshua) will call for to come up to Him, a Pretribulation Rapture of the church (Saints or elect) before the 7- years of Tribulation start, a Mid-Tribulation Rapture of the Church at (3.5 yrs) into the 7-years of Tribulation (Main Harvest) and a Pre-Wrath of the Remnant.

Chapter 13
The Bride of Christ and where to find in the Scriptures that support this?

There are people who believe Jesus Christ (Yeshua Hamashiach) is coming first to take His Bride, a real Bride prepared for Him alone. Scripture supports this belief:

In the book of Revelation it talks about Jesus' wife hath made herself ready. (Herself is plural). It talks about the marriage of the Lamb. Lamb = Jesus Christ (Yeshua Hamashiach)

Two scriptures pertaining to the belief that Jesus Christ (Yeshua Hamashiach) will have a Wedding Feast Ceremony for Himself and His Bride (One woman) as described in:

Revelation 19:7 [7] **Let us be glad and rejoice, and give honour to him: for the marriage of the Lamb is come, and his wife hath made herself ready. (Wife is singular)**

In verse 8   And to her was granted that she should be arrayed in fine linen clean and white: for the fine linen is the righteousness of saints. (She is singular)

In verse 9   and he saith unto me, Write Blessed are they which are called unto the marriage supper of the Lamb. And he saith unto me. These are the true sayings of God:

(They are plural).

In Luke 10 Martha is a type and shadow of the church and Mary is a type and shadow of the bride who is preparing herself to go up in the pre-tribulation rapture. Martha is preoccupied with HER own ministry of hospitality and doesn't recognize she should be hearing what Mary is hearing.

The Bride of Jesus Christ (Yeshua Hamashiach)

She is called the First Fruits.

Some believers think She is Raptured first before the 7-year Tribulation begins

In the original Aramaic text of the New Testament, there are scriptures found in **Matthew 25:1-13** referring to the bride and groom, saying that the virgins went out to meet the bridegroom and his bride. And though the highlighted words aren't found in the Greek text of Matthew, they are found in the Aramaic Targums, trusted more than the modern Greek text of the book of Matthew (Only). Christian writers tell us that Matthew wrote work in Aramaic or Hebrew, and it's apparent there were changes made either during or after translation into Greek in the early 2nd century BCE.

This text is preserved in ancient manuscripts, such as the Yonan Codex and Khabouris Codex, and some scientists date the Classical Syriac manuscript parchment of the codex back to the 10th century A.D. It contains the complete Peshitta New Testament. The inclusion of "And the bride" in this verse is consistent with the Aramaic text and is not found in most modern translations. The Greek translation of Matthew, which dates to around 70 CE, does not include this phrase, indicating that it is a feature of the Aramaic manuscripts. So, if Jesus (Yeshua) arrives with His bride, then it would indicate the virgins that are waiting are the invited guests.

Because the scripture refers to "she" (which is singular) when describing the bride, some people believe there is a woman somewhere here on earth, and she is going to be Jesus Christ (Yeshua Hamashiach) actual Bride. She will be brought up to the groom, Jesus Christ (Yeshua Hamashiach), who will remain in Heaven until the actual Rapture event for the believers of the church. Be it Pre- or Mid- Tribulation.

In the Bible:

God (Yahweh) brought Eve to Adam in **Genesis 2:22**

Rebekah was brought to Issac in **Genesis 24:61-67**

Woman at the well was brought to Jesus **John 4:5-8**

While He was on Jacob's property **(Jacob is a type & shadow of the Father)**

John 3:29 ²⁹He that hath the bride is the bridegroom: but the friend of the bridegroom, which

standeth and heareth him, rejoiceth greatly because of the bridegroom's voice: this my joy therefore is fulfilled.

No (Shout) will be made to the bride if and when she is brought up to Jesus (Yeshua).

More Bible scriptures that support there being an actual Bride of Jesus Christ (Yeshua Hamashiach):

Psalm 45: 9-14 [9] Kings' daughters were among thy honourable women: upon thy right hand did stand the queen in gold of Ophir. [10] Hearken, O daughter, and consider, and incline thine ear; forget also thine own people, and thy father's house; [11] So shall the king greatly desire thy beauty: for he is thy Lord; and worship thou him. [12] And the daughter of Tyre shall be there with a gift; even the rich among the people shall intreat thy favour. [13] The king's daughter is all glorious within: her clothing is of wrought gold. [14] She shall be brought unto the king in raiment of needlework: the virgins her companions that follow her shall be brought unto thee.

Isaiah 61:10 [10] I will greatly rejoice in the Lord, my soul shall be joyful in my God; for he hath clothed me with the garments of salvation, he hath covered me with the robe of righteousness, as a bridegroom decketh himself with ornaments, and as a bride adorneth herself with her jewels.

Joel 2:15 [15]Gather the people, sanctify the congregation, assemble the elders, gather the children, and those that suck the breasts: let the bridegroom go forth of his chamber, and the bride out of her closet.

Revelation 19: 7-9 [7] Let us be glad and rejoice, and give honour to him: for the marriage of. The Lamb is come, and his wife (singular) hath made herself ready. [8] And to her was granted that she should be arrayed in fine linen, clean and white: for the fine linen is the righteousness of saints. [9] And he saith unto me, Write, Blessed are they which are called unto the marriage supper of the Lamb. And he saith unto me, these are the true sayings of God.

Jeremiah 33:11 [11] I will greatly rejoice in the Lord, my soul shall be joyful in my God; for he hath clothed me with the garments of salvation, he hath covered me with the robe of righteousness, as a bridegroom decketh himself with ornaments, and as a bride adorneth herself with her jewels.

Revelation 22:17 [17] And the Spirit and the bride say, Come. And let him that heareth say, Come. And let him that is a thirst come. And whosoever will, let him take the water of life freely.

Most people believe the church is called the Bride of Christ (or the main harvest) and that Jesus (Yeshua) will rapture the believers, also called His sheep, right before the 7-year Tribulation starts.

There are scriptures to support a mid-tribulation rapture when the Antichrist (Beast) is revealed and the abomination of desolation is set up in the rebuilt 3rd temple when he will want to be worshipped as God worldwide, as mentioned in the Book of Daniel and the Book of Revelation.

Believers who worship Jesus Christ (Yeshua Hamashiach) in spirit and in truth every day are called the Church of Christ. People who make time for him every day, walk the narrow path, separate themselves from the world, pick up their cross daily, and repent when they sin, forgiving others, as they have been forgiven. Walking in love daily and forgiving others daily. Those who are in the world are not of it. Those who are looking and waiting for Jesus Christ's (Yeshua Hamashiach) return, his glorious appearing, as he says in his word.

Chapter 14
Scriptures that support a Pre-Tribulation Rapture Doctrine, the Remnant, and the Wrath of God (Yahweh) on the wicked to come

Key Scriptures Supporting the Pre-Tribulation Rapture of the Church Doctrine are as follows:

Matthew 24: 30-31 [30]And then shall appear the sign of the Son of man in heaven: and then shall all the tribes of the earth mourn, and they shall see the Son of man coming in the clouds of heaven with power and great glory. [31] And he shall send his angels with a great sound of a trumpet, and they shall gather together his elect from the four winds, from one end of heaven to the other.

1 Thessalonians 4: 15-17 [15] For this we say unto you by the word of the Lord, that we which are alive and

remain unto the coming of the Lord shall not prevent them which are asleep. [16] For the Lord himself shall descend from heaven with a shout, with the voice of the archangel, and with the trump of God: and the dead in Christ shall rise first: [17] Then we which are alive and remain shall be caught up together with them in the clouds, to meet the Lord in the air: and so shall we ever be with the Lord.

Revelation 3:10 [10]"Because you have kept my word about patient endurance, I will keep you from the hour of trial that is coming on the whole world, to try those who dwell on the earth. This verse is often interpreted as a promise that believers will be kept from the coming tribulation.

Revelation 12:5 [5] And she brought forth a man child, who was to rule all nations with a rod of iron: and her child was caught up unto God, and to his throne.

1 Thessalonians 5:9 [9]"For God has not destined us for wrath, but to obtain salvation through our Lord Jesus Christ."

This verse reassures believers that they are not appointed to experience the wrath associated with the tribulation.

John 14:2[2] "In my father's house are many rooms; if that were not so, would I have told you that I go to prepare a place for you? And if I go and prepare a place for you, I will come again and will take you to myself, that where I am you may be also."

This passage speaks to the promise of Jesus Christ (Yeshua Hamashiach) returning to take believers to be with Him.

People who believe in a Pre-Wrath snatching of the REMNANT (gleanings that fall from the trees and are bruised) believe the Remnant will remain in their mortal bodies but be snatched and taken to the safety of the "barn" while God (Yahweh) is pouring out His wrath during the Day of the Lord, which some say starts in the 6th year of the Tribulation, on the Day of Atonement, and lasts one year.

At the end of the age: God (Yahweh) pours out His wrath on the wicked according to what the parable of the wheat and tares says found in **(Matthew 13:24-30)**. The wheat represents the good and the tare's evil.

There are mid-tribulation rapture believers who believe Jesus Christ (Yeshua Hamashiach) will come at the midpoint of the 7-year tribulation, which is at the 3.5-year mark. The Antichrist will be revealed, aligning with the events described in **(Matthew 24:15)** regarding the **"abomination of desolation,"** when he sits in the rebuilt 3rd Temple, wanting to be worshipped as God (Yahweh) throughout the entire world.

Chapter 15
Scriptures that support a Mid-Tribulation Rapture Doctrine

The following verses discuss the coming of the Lord and the gathering of believers. They emphasize that certain events must occur before the rapture, including a falling away and the revelation of the "man of sin" (the Antichrist). This suggests that the rapture will happen after these events, aligning with the mid-tribulation perspective.

Key scriptures supporting the Mid-Tribulation Rapture Doctrine:

Revelation 11:15 [15] This verse describes the seventh trumpet sounding, which is often associated with the rapture occurring at the midpoint of the tribulation. It states, **"The kingdom of the world has become the kingdom of our Lord and of his Messiah, and he will reign for ever and ever."** This event marks a significant transition in the tribulation timeline.

2 Thessalonians 2:1-3 [1]"Now we beseech you, brethren, by the coming of our Lord Jesus Christ, and by our gathering together unto him, [2] That ye be not soon shaken in mind, or be troubled, neither by spirit, nor by word, nor by letter as from us, as that day of Christ is at hand. [3] Let no man deceive you by any means: for *that day shall not come*, except there comes a falling away first, and that man of sin be revealed, (the son of perdition.) [4] Who opposeth and exalteth himself above all that is called God, or that is worshipped: so that he as God sitteth in the temple of God, shewing himself that he is God.

2 Thessalonians 2: 8-12 [8] And then shall that Wicked be revealed, whom the Lord shall consume with the spirit of his mouth, and shall destroy with the brightness of his coming: [9] Even him, who's coming is after the working of Satan with all power and signs and lying wonders, [10] And with all deceivableness of unrighteousness in them that perish, because they received not the love of the truth, that they might be saved. [11] And for this cause God shall send them strong

delusion, that they should believe a lie: ¹² **That they all might be damned who believed not the truth, but had pleasure in unrighteousness.**

The Mid-Tribulation Resurrection Rapture Believers Who Worship Jesus Christ (Yeshua Hamashiach) in Spirit and in Truth (not in name only!) believe they will be Raptured at the midpoint. 3.5 years into the 7-year Tribulation, as the Bible teaches, we are Not appointed to Wrath.

1 Thessalonians 5: 9 ⁹ **For God hath not appointed us to wrath, but to obtain salvation by our Lord Jesus Christ.**

Note: Those 2 verses were taken out of the King James Bible! **At the Mid-Tribulation Rapture:**

There will be Gentiles and Jews that God will graft in at the midpoint (3.5 yrs) of the 7-year Tribulation. When they come to believe that Jesus Christ (Yeshua Hamashiach) died for our sins, was buried, and rose again on the third day, all according to the Scriptures. That Jesus Christ (Yeshua Hamashiach) is the Way, the truth, and the life, and no man comes to the Father (Yahweh) except through Him. He's our Lord and Savior.

It says in:

Romans 11: 23 [23] **And they also if they do not continue in their unbelief will be grafted in for God is Able to graft them in again.**

Interesting how the 15th and 16th verses below in 2 Corinthians 13: 15-16 were taken out of the Bible. The KJV doesn't have these scriptures either. These verses are regarding the Jewish people being grafted in if they turn to Jesus Christ (Yeshua Hamashiach).

2 Corinthians 13:15-16 [15] **in the (Nasib) Bible reads: "But to this day whenever Moses is read, a veil lies over their heart: but whenever a person turns to the Lord, the veil is taken away."**

Chapter 16
The Gleanings (The Remnant), Scriptures supporting a post-tribulation ingathering General Rapture Scriptures

Gleanings are called the Remnant. They are snatched by the reapers at Pre-Wrath Taken to the barn for safety, while remaining in their mortal bodies.

The parable of the wheat and tares:

Matthew 13: 25-30 [25] Another parable put He forth unto them, saying, the kingdom of heaven is likened unto a man which sowed good seed in his field: [25] But while men slept, his enemy came and sowed tares among the wheat, and went his way. [26] But when the blade was sprung up, and brought forth fruit, then appeared the tares also. [27] So the servants of the householder came and said unto him, Sir, didst not

thou sow good seed in thy field? from whence then hath it tares? [28] **He said unto them, an enemy hath done this. The servants said unto him, wilt thou then that we go and gather them up?** [29] **But he said, Nay; lest while ye gather up the tares, ye root up also the wheat with them.** [30] **Let both grow together until the harvest: and in the time of harvest I will say to the reapers, gather ye together first the tares, and bind them in bundles to burn them: but gather the wheat into my barn.**

God (Yahweh) will remove the Remnant out of the crossfire to destroy the wicked. They are snatched by the reapers and taken to the barn for safety and remain in their mortal bodies.

Some people believe in The Post – Tribulation ingathering

This is towards the end of the 7-year Tribulation.

Jesus Christ (Yeshua Hamashiach) says he will shorten the time, or no flesh will be saved.

When the 7-year Tribulation is over, the surviving Jews and Gentiles will return to their nations. It is a process and journey of the Mortal remnant, that travels back to their nation after the dust settles.

The Book of Ruth is prophesying Post – Tribulation events.

Exodus 23:16 and Exodus 34:22 mentions the Feast of Ingathering at the end of the year.

The following are some general Rapture Scriptures found In the KJV Bible

Daniel 9:27 [27] **And he shall confirm the covenant with many for one week. 7 days is = to 7 years: in the midst of the week 3.5 years, he shall cause the sacrifice and the oblation to cease, and for the overspreading of abominations he shall make it desolate, even until the consummation, and that determination shall be poured upon the desolate.**

1 Thessalonians 5: 1-3 [1] **But of the times and the seasons, brethren, ye have no need that I write unto you.** [2] **For yourselves know perfectly that the day of**

the Lord so cometh as a thief in the night. [3] For when they shall say, Peace and safety; then sudden destruction cometh upon them, as travail upon a woman with child; and they shall not escape.

Revelation 1:7 [7] Behold, He is coming with clouds and EVERY EYE WILL SEE HIM, even they who pierced Him. and all kindreds of the earth shall wail because of him. Even so, Amen.

Hebrews 11:6 [6] And without faith it is impossible to please Yah "Our Heavenly Father" because anyone who comes to him must Believe that he exists and that he rewards those who EARNESTLY seek him.

Titus 2:13 [13]*Looking for that blessed hope, and *the glorious appearing* of the great Yah and our Savior Yahushua.

Luke 12:37 [37]Blessed are those servants, whom Jesus Christ (Yeshua Hamashiach), when he cometh shall find watching verily I say unto you, that he shall gird himself, and make them sit down to meat, and will come forth and serve them. [38] And if he shall come in the second watch, or come in the third watch, and find them so, blessed are those servants. [39] And this know, that if the goodman of the house had known what hour the thief would come, he would have watched, and not have suffered his house to be broken through.

Revelation 3:10 [10] Because thou hast kept the word of my patience, I also will keep thee from the hour of temptation, which shall come upon all the world, to try them that dwell upon the earth.

Luke 21:34 [34] And take heed to yourselves, lest at any time your hearts be overcharged with surfeiting, and drunkenness, and cares of this life, and so that day come upon you unawares [36] Watch ye therefore, and pray always, that **ye may be accounted worthy to escape all these things that shall come to pass**, and to stand before the Son of man.

2 Corinthians 6:17 [17] "Wherefore come out from among them and be ye separate, saith the Lord, and touch not the unclean thing: and I will receive you."

Matthew 7:13-14 [13] Enter ye in at the strait gate: for wide is the gate, and broad is the way, that leadeth to destruction, and many there be which go in there at: [14] Because strait is the gate, and narrow is the way, which leadeth unto life, and few there be that find it.

God's, (Yahweh's) angels will come for people who are obedient to God the Father's (Yahweh's) word, Passionate about Jesus Christ (Yeshua Hamashiach). They are the ones who will be caught up in the clouds.

Luke 21: 25-28 [25] And there shall be signs in the sun, and in the moon, and in the stars: and upon the earth distress of nations with perplexity: the sea and the waves roaring: [26] Men's hearts failing them for fear, and for looking after those things which are coming on the earth: for the powers of heaven shall be shaken. [27] And then shall they see the Son of man coming in a cloud with power and great glory. [28] And when these things begin to come to pass, then *look up*, and lift up your heads; for your redemption draweth nigh. (Look Up, Lift your HEADS!! Your RESCUE!! or REDEEMER draws near).

St. Mark 13: 26-27 [26] And then shall they see the son of man coming in the clouds with great power and glory. [27] And then shall he send his angels, and shall gather his elect from the four winds, from the uttermost part of the earth to the uttermost part of heaven.

1 Thessalonians 1: 10 [10] And to WAIT for his SON from heaven, whom he raised from the dead, even Jesus, which delivered us from the wrath to come.

1 Thessalonians 4:16-17 [16] For Jesus Christ (Yeshua Hamashiach) himself shall descend from heaven with a shout, with the voice of the archangel, and with the trump of God (Yahweh): and the dead in Jesus Christ (Yeshua Hamashiach), shall rise first: [17] Then we which are alive and remain shall be caught up together with them in the clouds, to meet the Lord in the air: and so shall we ever be with the Lord. [18] Wherefore comfort one another with these words.

1Thessalonians 5: 6-9 [6] Therefore let us not sleep, as do others; but let us watch and be sober. [7] For they that sleep in the night; and they that be drunken are drunken in the night. But let us, who are of the day, be sober, putting on the breastplate of faith and love; and for an helmet, the hope of salvation. [9] For God, (Yahweh) hath not appointed us to wrath, but to obtain salvation by our Lord Jesus Christ (Yeshua Hamashiach).

1 Corinthians 15: 51-52 [51]Behold, I shew you a mystery, we shall not all sleep, but we shall all be changed. [52]In a moment, in the twinkling of an eye, at the last trump: for the trumpet shall sound, and the dead shall be raised incorruptible and we shall be changed.

Ephesians 5:27 [27] That he might present it to himself a glorious church, not having spot or wrinkle, or any such thing but that it should be holy and without blemish.

2 Peter 3: 3-4 [3] Knowing this first, that there shall come in the last days scoffers, walking after their own lusts, [4]And saying, where is the promise of his coming? for since the fathers fell asleep, all things continue as they were from the beginning of the creation.

Peter 3:9 [9]Jesus Christ, (Yeshua Hamashiach) is not slack concerning his promise, as some men count slackness, but is longsuffering to us-ward, *not willing that any should perish*but that all should come to repentance. *Repent of any sins if we do* *Forgiving others as we have been forgiven* If we make Yeshua our Lord & Savior of our life He will provide and take care of us. By us Having *Faith* in Him in all situations we face. While having no fear!

Revelation 3:10 [10] Because thou hast kept the word of my patience, *I also will keep thee from the hour of temptation, which shall come upon all the world* to try them that dwell upon the earth. [11]Behold, I come quickly: hold that fast which thou hast, that no man takes thy crown.

Revelation 3:16 [6]So then because thou art lukewarm, and neither cold nor hot, I will spue thee out of my mouth.

Revelation 13:6 [6] And he opened his mouth in blasphemy against God, to blaspheme his name and his tabernacle, and them that dwell in heaven.

Revelation 19:7 [7] Let us be glad and rejoice, and give honour to him: for the marriage of the Lamb has come, and his wife hath made herself ready. [8]And to her was granted that she should be arrayed in fine linen, clean and white: for the fine linen is the righteousness of saints.

Revelation 19:14 [14] And the armies (the raptured saints) which were *in heaven followed him Jesus Christ (Yeshua Hamashiach) upon white horses, clothed in fine linen, white and clean.*

2 Thessalonians 2:3 [3] Let no man deceive you by any means: for that day shall not come, except there comes

a *falling away* first, and that man of sin be revealed, the son of perdition; *Falling Away* (Departing)

Jeremiah 30:7 [7] Alas! For that day is great, so that none is like it, it is even the time of Jacob's Trouble, but he shall be saved out of it. (Those who worship Jesus Christ (Yeshua Hamashiach) in spirit and in truth)

1 Thessalonians 5:23 [23] And the very God of peace sanctify you wholly; and I pray God your *whole spirit and soul and body be preserved blameless* unto the coming of our Lord Jesus Christ (Yeshua Hamashiach) Righteous and repentant people when they sin, Be Ready, Be Holy.

1Thessalonians 1: 7-12 [7]And to you who are troubled rest with us, when the Lord Jesus shall be revealed from heaven with his mighty angels, [8]In flaming fire taking vengeance on them that know not God, and that obey not the gospel of our Lord Jesus Christ: [9] Who shall be punished with everlasting destruction from the presence of the Lord, and from the glory of his power; ¹⁰ When he shall come to be glorified in his saints, (Believers including both Jew and Gentile) and to be *admired in all them that believe* (because our testimony among you was believed) in that day. ¹¹ Wherefore also *we pray always for you, that our God would count you worthy of this calling, and fulfill all the good pleasure of his goodness, and the work of faith with power*: ¹² That the name of our Lord Jesus Christ may be glorified in you, and ye in him, according to the grace of our God and the Lord Jesus Christ.

Luke 21:34 ³⁴ And take heed to yourselves, lest at any time your hearts be overcharged with surfeiting, and drunkenness, and cares of this life, and so that day come upon you unawares ³⁶ Watch ye therefore, and pray always, that *ye may be accounted worthy to escape all these things that shall come to pass* and to stand before the Son of man.

Chapter 17
The First and Second Coming of Jesus Christ (Yeshua Hamashiach)

The end of the Tribulation and the Believers who believe we should go through the wrath

To reiterate the First and Second Coming of Jesus Christ (Yeshua Hamashiach).

1st Coming of Jesus Christ (Yeshua Hamashiach): Jesus (Yeshua) comes in the clouds, and His Angels gather his elect, the bride, from the 4 corners of the Earth in what's called a Rapture, a gathering, a (Harpazo) in Greek.

Matthew 24: 30-31 [30]And then shall appear the sign of the Son of man in heaven: and then shall all the tribes of the earth mourn, and they shall see the Son of man coming in the clouds of heaven with power and great glory. [31] And he shall send his angels with a great sound of a trumpet, and they shall gather together his

elect from the four winds, from one end of heaven to the other.

2nd Coming of Jesus Christ (Yeshua Hamashiach) there are some who believe He will also come 3.5 years into the 7-year Tribulation, at the mid-point when the Great Tribulation begins. This is when The Beast of Revelation (Anti-Christ) will sit in the rebuilt 3rd Temple in Jerusalem claiming himself to be God and demanding Global Worship. The Mark of the Beast will be given at this time, either a mark in your right hand or forehead.

Revelation 13: 16 [16] And he causeth all: both small and great rich and poor free and bond, to receive a mark in their right hand or in their foreheads: [17] And that no man might buy or sell save he that had the mark, or the name of the Beast, or the number of his name.

The end of the 7-year Tribulation is when Jesus Christ (Yeshua Hamashiach) comes back to EARTH with the Raptured Saints. The armies that were in heaven will follow him upon white horses, clothed in fine linen, white and clean, to the Battle of Armageddon.

Revelation 19: 13-14 [13] **And he was clothed with a vesture dipped in blood: and his name is called The Word of God (Jesus)** [14] **And the armies which were in heaven followed him upon white horses, clothed in fine linen, white and clean.**

Clothed in linen, white and clean, is the righteousness of the saints! The Believers who made themselves ready, being repentant and obedient, making Jesus Lord and Savior of their lives.

The end of the 7-year Tribulation is the establishment of Jesus Christ's (Yeshua Hamashiach's) kingdom, His coronation as King, His marriage to His Bride, and the ultimate judgment of humanity. Believers who worship Jesus Christ (Yeshua Hamashiach) are assured of their place in the Millennial Kingdom, while non-believers face eternal separation from God (Yahweh). This period is characterized by hope for the faithful and justice for the unrighteous.

There are believers who believe we shouldn't take the mark of the beast when given and have to endure to the end of the Tribulation in order to be saved and raptured.

They are ignoring the previous raptures, and scripture tells us we are not appointed to wrath.

Mark 13:35 ³⁵ Watch ye therefore: for ye know not when the master of the house cometh, at even, or at even, or at midnight, or at the cockcrowing, or in the morning: ³⁶ Lest coming suddenly he finds you sleeping, ³⁷And what I say unto you I say unto all. Watch!

Luke 21:34-36 ³⁶And take heed to yourselves, lest at any time your hearts be overcharged with surfeiting, and drunkenness, and cares of this life, and so that day come upon you unawares. ³⁶ Watch ye therefore, and pray always, that ye may be accounted worthy to escape all these things that shall come to pass, and to stand before the Son of man.

Hebrews 9:28 ²⁸ So Christ was once offered to bear the sins of many: and unto them that look for him shall he appear the second time without sin unto salvation.

Chapter 18
Not everyone will be taken!

7 Scriptures supporting those who cannot inherit the Kingdom of God

When the rapture (Harpazo) takes place, not every believer or follower of Jesus Christ (Yeshua Hamashiach) will be taken, because either they were lukewarm Christians in name only, or Christians that didn't truly believe Jesus Christ (Yeshua Hamashiach) was coming to rapture His believers that worship Him in Spirit and in Truth, or they weren't looking spiritually for Him, or they didn't prepare themselves. Maybe their hearts weren't aligned, or their lives are not marked by holiness. Jesus Christ (Yeshu Hamashiach) also said in His Word:

Matthew 7: 21-23 [21] Not everyone that saith unto me, Lord, Lord, shall enter into the kingdom of heaven: but he that doeth the will of my Father which is in heaven. [22] Many will say to me in that day, Lord, Lord,

have we not prophesied in thy name? and in thy name have cast out devils? And in thy name done many wonderful works? [23] And then will I profess unto them, I never knew you: depart from me, ye that work iniquity.

Matthew 7: 13-14 [13] Enter ye in at the strait gate: for wide is the gate, and broad is the way, that leadeth to destruction, and many there be which go in thereat: [14] Because strait is the gate, and narrow is the way, which leadeth unto life, and few there be that find it.

Some believe that those who are not preparing themselves for the next step of ministry will go up at mid-trib. It isn't that God (Yahweh) loves any of us more than the others; it's a matter of who is preparing themselves. God (Yahweh) has invited all of us to be a part of the rapture, but not all Christians are truly interested in the Word or a solid relationship with Jesus (Yeshua). They are saved, but they need a little more time to mature!

7 Scriptures in the New Testament: You cannot inherit the Kingdom of Heaven.

1 Corinthians 6: 9-10 [9] Know ye not that the unrighteous shall not inherit the kingdom of God? Be not be deceived: neither fornicators, nor idolaters, nor adulterers, nor effeminate, nor abusers of themselves with mankind, [10] Nor thieves, nor covetous, nor drunkards, nor revilers, nor extortioners: shall inherit the Kingdom of God.

Galatians 5:19 [19] The acts of the flesh are obvious: sexual immortality, impurity and debauchery, idolatry and witchcraft, hatred, discord, jealousy, fits of rage, selfish ambition, dissensions, factions and envy drunkenness.

2 Chronicles 15:2 [2] The Lord is with you, while ye be with him. And if ye seek him he will be found of you, but if ye forsake him he will forsake you.

Ephesians 5:5 [5] For of this you can be sure: No immoral, impure of greedy person such a person is an idolater has any inheritance in the Kingdom of Christ and of God Let no one deceive you with empty words, for because of such things "God's wrath comes on those who are Disobedient."

Matthew: 7:22-23 [22] On that day many will say to me, Lord, Lord, did we not prophesy in your name, and cast out demons in your name and do many mighty works in your name? And then will I declare to them. I never knew you depart from me, you workers of lawlessness.

Ephesians 4:18 [18]Having the understanding darkened being alienated from the life of God through the ignorance that is in them, because of the Blindness of their Heart.

Colossians 2:8 [8] Beware lest any man spoil you, through philosophy and vain deceit, after the tradition of men, after the rudiments of the world, and NOT after Christ.

God (Yahweh) gets All the glory, honor, and praise for All things, EVERYTHING! For He is our one true God (Yahweh), Maker of heaven and earth, of all creation. We come to Him through our one and only Mediator, and that is His Son, Jesus Christ (Yeshua Hamashiach), whom He is well pleased with. The King of Kings, who will rule from the New Jerusalem that will come down from heaven in the 1000-year Millennium, after the last Battle of Armageddon takes place and the 7 years of Tribulation end.

In the end, there is hope for everyone, because God is not a respecter of persons. He accepts all of those, regardless of what race, nation, or ethnic group they might belong to, if they are genuinely seeking God the Father (Yahweh) with all their heart and mind and soul.

In Acts 2:9 [9]Elamites (modern-day Iranians) were peacefully assembled in Jerusalem on the day of Pentecost, when the Holy Spirit was given to the New Testament Church. And when Jesus Christ (Yeshua Hamashiach) rules this world from Jerusalem, all nations, including Elamites, will ultimately flow to Him to learn God's (Yahweh's) ways (Isaiah 2:1-4).

Chapter 19
99 Bible verses supporting the Millennium after the Tribulation

99 Bible verses related to *The Millennium* from the KJV, by Relevance

Here are 99 Bible verses about the 1000-year millennium that takes place after the 7 years of Tribulation and after the Battle of Armageddon, where Jesus Christ (Yeshua Hamashiach) will rule and reign on earth. Scriptures from both the Old and New Testaments of the Holy Bible, King James Version, arranged from most to least relevant.

Revelation 20:1-15

[1] And I saw an angel come down from heaven, having the key of the bottomless pit and a great chain in his hand. [2] And he laid hold on the dragon, that old serpent, which is the Devil, and Satan, and bound him

a thousand years, ³ And cast him into the bottomless pit, and shut him up, and set a seal upon him, that he should deceive the nations no more, till the thousand years should be fulfilled:

Revelation 20:4

⁴ And I saw thrones, and they sat upon them, and judgment was given unto them: and I saw the souls of them that were beheaded for the witness of Jesus, and for the word of God, and which had not worshipped the beast, neither his image, neither had received his mark upon their foreheads, or in their hands; and they lived and reigned with Christ a thousand years.

Daniel 2:44

⁴⁴ And in the days of these kings shall the God of heaven set up a kingdom, which shall never be destroyed: and the kingdom shall not be left to other people, but it shall break in pieces and consume all these kingdoms, and it shall stand forever.

Matthew 19:28

28 And Jesus said unto them, Verily I say unto you, that ye which have followed me, in the regeneration when the Son of man shall sit in the throne of his glory, ye also shall sit upon twelve thrones, judging the twelve tribes of Israel.

Daniel 7:27

27 And the kingdom and dominion, and the greatness of the kingdom under the whole heaven, shall be given to the people of the saints of the Highest, whose kingdom is an everlasting kingdom, and all dominions shall serve and obey him.

Isaiah 65:25

25 The wolf and the lamb shall feed together, and the lion shall eat straw like the bullock: and dust shall be the serpent's meat. They shall not hurt nor destroy in all my holy mountain, saith the Lord.

Revelation 20:7

7And when the thousand years are expired, Satan shall be loosed out of his prison,...

Revelation 20:5

5 But the rest of the dead lived not again until the thousand years were finished. This is the first resurrection.

Daniel 7:13-14

13 I saw in the night visions, and, behold, one like the Son of man came with the clouds of heaven, and came to the Ancient of days, and they brought him near before him. 14 And there was given him dominion, and glory, and a kingdom, that all people, nations, and languages, should serve him: his dominion is an everlasting dominion, which shall not pass away, and his kingdom that which shall not be destroyed.

Zechariah 14:16

16 And it shall come to pass, that every one that is left of all the nations which came against Jerusalem

shall even go up from year to year to worship the King, the Lord of hosts, and to keep the feast of tabernacles.

Isaiah 9: 6-7

[6] For unto us a child is born, unto us a son is given: and the government shall be upon his shoulder: and his name shall be called Wonderful, Counsellor, The mighty God, The everlasting Father, The Prince of Peace. [7] Of the increase of his government and peace there shall be no end, upon the throne of David, and upon his kingdom, to order it, and to establish it with judgment and with justice from henceforth even forever.

Luke 1:32-33

[32] He shall be great, and shall be called the Son of the Highest: and the Lord God shall give unto him the throne of his father David: [33] And he shall reign over the house of Jacob forever; and of his kingdom there shall be no end.

Isaiah 11:1-16

¹ And there shall come forth a rod out of the stem of Jesse, and a Branch shall grow out of his roots: ² And the spirit of the Lord shall rest upon him, the spirit of wisdom and understanding, the spirit of counsel and might, the spirit of knowledge and of the fear of the Lord; ³ And shall make him of quick understanding in the fear of the Lord: and he shall not judge after the sight of his ...

Psalm 2: 6-9

⁶ Yet have I set my king upon my holy hill of Zion. ⁷ I will declare the decree: the Lord hath said unto me, thou art my Son; this day have I begotten thee. ⁸ Ask of me, and I shall give thee the heathen for thine inheritance, and the uttermost parts of the earth for thy possession. ⁹ Thou shalt break them with a rod of iron; thou shalt dash them in pieces like a potters vessel.

Revelation 19: 11-21

^{11} And I saw heaven opened, and behold a white horse; and he that sat upon him was called Faithful and True, and in righteousness he doth judge and make war. ^{12} His eyes were as a flame of fire, and on his head were many crowns; and he had a name written, that no man knew, but he himself. ^{13} And he was clothed with a vesture dipped in blood: and his name is called The Word of God...

Isaiah 11:4

4But with righteousness shall he judge the poor, and reprove with equity for the meek of the earth: and he shall smite the earth: with the rod of his mouth, and with the breath of his lips shall he slay the wicked.

Zechariah 9:10

^{10} And I will cut off the chariot from Ephraim, and the horse from Jerusalem, and the battle bow shall be cut off: and he shall speak peace unto the heathen: and his dominion shall be from sea even to sea, and from the river even to the ends of the earth.

Zechariah 9:9

⁹ Rejoice greatly, O daughter of Zion; shout, O daughter of Jerusalem: behold, thy King cometh unto thee: he is just, and having salvation; lowly, and riding upon an ass, and upon a colt the foal of an ass.

Isaiah 11:9

⁹ They shall not hurt nor destroy in all my holy mountain: for the earth shall be full of the knowledge of the Lord, as the waters cover the sea.

Revelation 20:6

⁶ Blessed and holy is he that hath part in the first resurrection: on such the second death hath no power, but they shall be priests of God and of Christ, and shall reign with him a thousand years.

Revelation 19:1-21

¹ And after these things I heard a great voice of much people in heaven, saying, Alleluia; Salvation, and glory, and honour, and power, unto the Lord our God: ² For true and righteous are his judgments: for he hath judged the great whore, which did corrupt the earth

with her fornication, and hath avenged the blood of his servants at her hand. [3] And again they said, Alleluia And her smoke rose up ...

Isaiah 2:2-4

[2] And it shall come to pass in the last days, that the mountain of the Lord's house shall be established in the top of the mountains, and shall be exalted above the hills; and all nations shall flow unto it. [3] And many people shall go and say, come ye, and let us go up to the mountain of the Lord, to the house of the God of Jacob; and he will teach us of his ways, and we will walk in his paths: for out of Zion shall go forth ...

Zechariah 8:3

[3] Thus saith the Lord; I am returned unto Zion, and will dwell in the midst of Jerusalem: and Jerusalem shall be called a city of truth; and the mountain of the Lord of hosts the holy mountain.

Revelation 20:3

³ And cast him into the bottomless pit, and shut him up, and set a seal upon him, that he should deceive the nations no more, till the thousand years should be fulfilled: and after that he must be loosed a little season.

Revelation 5:10

¹⁰ And hast made us unto our God kings and priests: and we shall reign on the earth.

Zechariah 14:4

⁴ And his feet shall stand in that day upon the mount of Olives, which is before Jerusalem on the east, and the mount of Olives shall cleave in the midst thereof toward the east and toward the west, and there shall be a very great valley; and half of the mountain shall remove toward the north, and half of it toward the south.

Revelation 20:1-7

¹ And I saw an angel come down from heaven, having the key of the bottomless pit and a great chain in his hand. ² And he laid hold on the dragon, that old

serpent, which is the Devil, and Satan, and bound him a thousand years, [3] And cast him into the bottomless pit, and shut him up, and set a seal upon him, that he should deceive the nations no more, till the thousand years should be fulfilled...

John 3:16

[16] For God so loved the world, that he gave his only begotten Son, that whosoever believeth in him should not perish, but have everlasting life.

John 1:1

[1] In the beginning was the Word, and the Word was with God, and the Word was God.

Daniel 7:14

[14] And there was given him dominion, and glory, and a kingdom, that all people, nations, and languages, should serve him: his dominion is an everlasting dominion, which shall not pass away, and his kingdom that which shall not be destroyed.

Zechariah 14:16-17

^{16} And it shall come to pass, that every one that is left of all the nations which came against Jerusalem shall even go up from year to year to worship the King, the Lord of hosts, and to keep the feast of tabernacles. ^{17} And it shall be, that whoso will not come up of all the families of the earth unto Jerusalem to worship the King, the Lord of hosts, even upon them shall be no rain.

John 16:33

^{33} These things I have spoken unto you, that in me ye might have peace. In the world ye shall have tribulation: but be of good cheer; I have overcome the world.

Micah 4:1-8

^{1} But in the last days it shall come to pass, that the mountain of the house of the Lord shall be established in the top of the mountains, and it shall be exalted above the hills; and people shall flow unto it. ^{2} And many nations shall come, and say, Come, and let us go up to the mountain of the Lord, and to the house of

the God of Jacob; and he will teach us of his ways, and
we will walk in his paths: for the law shall go forth...

Isaiah 11:3-5

[3] And shall make him of quick understanding in the
fear of the Lord: and he shall not judge after the sight
of his eyes, neither reprove after the hearing of his
ears: [4] But with righteousness shall he judge the poor,
and reprove with equity for the meek of the earth: and
he shall smite the earth: with the rod of his mouth,
and with the breath of his lips shall he slay the
wicked...

Micah 5:2-5

[2] But thou, Bethlehem Ephratah, though thou be
little among the thousands of Judah, yet out of thee
shall he come forth unto me that is to be ruler in Israel;
whose goings forth have been from of old, from
everlasting. [3] Therefore will he give them up, until the
time that she which travaileth hath brought forth:
then the remnant of his brethren shall return unto the
children of Israel...

Daniel 2:35

³⁵ Then was the iron, the clay, the brass, the silver, and the gold, broken to pieces together, and became like the chaff of the summer threshing floors; and the wind carried them away, that no place was found for them: and the stone that smote the image became a great mountain, and filled the whole earth.

Isaiah 40:1-11

¹ Comfort ye, comfort ye my people, saith your God. ² Speak ye comfortably to Jerusalem, and cry unto her, that her warfare is accomplished, that her iniquity is pardoned: for she hath received of the Lord's hand double for all her sins. ³ The voice of him that crieth in the wilderness, prepare ye the way of the Lord, make straight in the desert a highway for our God...

Isaiah 11:1-10

¹And there shall come forth a rod out of the stem of Jesse, and a Branch shall grow out of his roots: ² And the spirit of the Lord shall rest upon him, the spirit of

wisdom and understanding, the spirit of counsel and might, the spirit of knowledge and of the fear of the Lord; [3] And shall make him of quick understanding in the fear of the Lord: and he shall not judge after the sight of his ...

Psalm 72:9-11

[9] They that dwell in the wilderness shall bow before him; and his enemies shall lick the dust. [10] The kings of Tarshish and of the isles shall bring presents: the kings of Sheba and Seba shall offer gifts. [11] Yea, all kings shall fall down before him: all nations shall serve him.

Isaiah 65:20

[20] There shall be no more thence an infant of days, nor an old man that hath not filled his days: for the child shall die an hundred years old; but the sinner being an hundred years old shall be accursed.

Revelation 20:12

^{12} And I saw the dead, small and great, stand before God; and the books were opened: and another book was opened, which is the book of life: and the dead were judged out of those things which were written in the books, according to their works.

Revelation 20:11

^{11} And I saw a great white throne, and him that sat on it, from whose face the earth and the heaven fled away; and there was found no place for them.

Matthew 25:31-46

^{31} When the Son of man shall come in his glory, and all the holy angels with him, then shall he sit upon the throne of his glory: ^{32} And before him shall be gathered all nations: and he shall separate them one from another, as a shepherd divideth his sheep from the goats: ^{33} And he shall set the sheep on his right hand, but the goats on the left. ^{34} Then shall the...

Micah 4:1-2

^{1} But in the last days it shall come to pass, that the mountain of the house of the Lord shall be established in the top of the mountains, and it shall be exalted above the hills; and people shall flow unto it. ^{2} And many nations shall come, and say, come, and let us go up to the mountain of the Lord, and to the house of the God of Jacob; and he will teach us of his ways, and we will walk in his paths: for the law shall go forth...

Isaiah 52:7-15

^{7} How beautiful upon the mountains are the feet of him that bringeth good tidings, that publisheth peace; that bringeth good tidings of good, that publisheth salvation; that saith unto Zion, Thy God reigneth! ^{8} Thy watchmen shall lift up the voice; with the voice together shall they sing: for they shall see eye to eye, when the Lord shall bring again Zion. ^{9} Break forth into joy, sing together, ye...

Isaiah 32:1

[1] Behold, a king shall reign in righteousness, and princes shall rule in judgment.

Isaiah 2:4

[4] And he shall judge among the nations, and shall rebuke many people: and they shall beat their swords into plowshares, and their spears into pruning hooks: nation shall not lift up sword against nation, neither shall they learn war any more.

Isaiah 2:1-3

[1] The word that Isaiah the son of Amoz saw concerning Judah and Jerusalem. [2] And it shall come to pass in the last days, that the mountain of the Lord's house shall be established in the top of the mountains, and shall be exalted above the hills; and all nations shall flow unto it. [3] And many people shall go and say, come ye, and let us go up to the mountain of the Lord, to the house of the God

Psalm 72:8

⁸ He shall have dominion also from sea to sea, and from the river unto the ends of the earth.

Revelation 19:16

¹⁶ And he hath on his vesture and on his thigh a name written, King of Kings, And Lord of Lords.

Hosea 3:5

⁵ Afterward shall the children of Israel return, and seek the Lord their God, and David their king; and shall fear the Lord and his goodness in the latter days.

Ezekiel 37:24-25

²⁴ And David my servant shall be king over them; and they all shall have one shepherd: they shall also walk in my judgments, and observe my statutes, and do them. ²⁵ And they shall dwell in the land that I have given unto Jacob my servant, wherein your fathers have dwelt; and they shall dwell therein, even they, and their children, and their children's children for ever: and my servant David shall be their prince forever.

Ezekiel 34:23-24

[23] And I will set up one shepherd over them, and he shall feed them, even my servant David; he shall feed them, and he shall be their shepherd. [24] And I the Lord will be their God, and my servant David a prince among them; I the Lord have spoken it.

Jeremiah 30:9

[9] But they shall serve the Lord their God, and David their king, whom I will raise up unto them.

Isaiah 42:3-4

[3] A bruised reed shall he not break, and the smoking flax shall he not quench: he shall bring forth judgment unto truth. [4] He shall not fail nor be discouraged, till he has set judgment in the earth: and the isles shall wait for his law.

Isaiah 35:5-6

⁵ Then the eyes of the blind shall be opened, and the ears of the deaf shall be unstopped. ⁶ Then shall the lame man leap as an heart, and the tongue of the dumb sing: for in the wilderness shall waters break out, and streams in the desert.

2 Samuel 7:16

¹⁶ And thine house and thy kingdom shall be established for ever before thee: thy throne shall be established forever.

Revelation 20:1-3

¹ And I saw an angel come down from heaven, having the key of the bottomless pit and a great chain in his hand. ² And he laid hold on the dragon, that old serpent, which is the Devil, and Satan, and bound him a thousand years, ³ And cast him into the bottomless pit, and shut him up, and set a seal upon him, that he should deceive the nations no more, till the thousand years should be fulfilled:

Revelation 11:1-19

^{1} And there was given me a reed like unto a rod: and the angel stood, saying, Rise, and measure the temple of God, and the altar, and them that worship therein. ^{2} But the court which is without the temple leaves out, and measures it not; for it is given unto the Gentiles: and the holy city shall they tread under foot forty and two months. ^{3} And I will give power unto my two witnesses, and they shall...

Revelation 1:1

^{1} The Revelation of Jesus Christ, which God gave unto him, to shew unto his servants' things which must shortly come to pass; and he sent and signified it by his angel unto his servant John:

Luke 19:14

^{14} But his citizens hated him, and sent a message after him, saying, we will not have this man to reign over us.

Mark 15:12-13

^{12} And Pilate answered and said again unto them, what will ye then that I shall do unto him whom ye call the King of the Jews? ^{13} And they cried out again, Crucify him.

Matthew 27:37

^{37} And set up over his head his accusation written, This Is Jesus the King of The Jews.

Jeremiah 33:19-21

^{19} And the word of the Lord came unto Jeremiah, saying, ^{20} Thus saith the Lord; If ye can break my covenant of the day, and my covenant of the night, and that there should not be day and night in their season; ^{21} Then may also my covenant be broken with David my servant, that he should not have a son to reign upon his throne; and with the Levites the priests, my ministers.

Jeremiah 33:15-17

¹⁵ In those days, and at that time, will I cause the Branch of righteousness to grow up unto David; and he shall execute judgment and righteousness in the land. ¹⁶ In those days shall Judah be saved, and Jerusalem shall dwell safely: and this is the name wherewith she shall be called, The Lord our righteousness. ¹⁷ For thus saith the Lord; David shall never want a man to sit upon the throne of the house of Isreal;

Isaiah 55:4

⁴ Behold, I have given him for a witness to the people, a leader and commander to the people.

Isaiah 24:23

²³ Then the moon shall be confounded, and the sun ashamed, when the Lord of hosts shall reign in mount Zion, and in Jerusalem, and before his ancients gloriously.

Song of Solomon 3:1-11

^{1} By night on my bed I sought him whom my soul loveth: I sought him, but I found him not. ^{2} I will rise now, and go about the city in the streets, and in the broad ways I will seek him whom my soul loveth: I sought him, but I found him not. ^{3} The watchmen that go about the city found me: to whom I said, Saw ye him whom my soul loveth? ^{4} It was but a little that I...

Psalm 89:20-37

^{20} I have found David my servant; with my holy oil have I anointed him: ^{21} With whom my hand shall be established: mine arm also shall strengthen him. ^{22} The enemy shall not exact upon him; nor the son of wickedness afflict him. ^{23} And I will beat down his foes before his face, and plague them that hate him...

Psalm 2:10-12

^{10} Be wise now therefore, O ye kings: be instructed, ye judges of the earth. ^{11} Serve the Lord with fear, and rejoice with trembling. ^{12} Kiss the Son, lest he be angry, and ye perish from the way, when his wrath is kindled but a little. Blessed are all they that put their trust in him.

Psalm 2:9

[9] Thou shalt break them with a rod of iron; thou shalt dash them in pieces like a potter's vessel.

John 14:6

[6] Jesus saith unto him, I am the way, the truth, and the life: no man cometh unto the Father, but by me.

Ezekiel 20:33-38

[33] As I live, saith the Lord God, surely with a mighty hand, and with a stretched out arm, and with fury poured out, will I rule over you: [34] And I will bring you out from the people, and will gather you out of the countries wherein ye are scattered, with a mighty hand, and with a stretched out arm, and with fury poured out. [35] And I will bring you into the wilderness of the people, and there will I...

Isaiah 16:5

[5] And in mercy shall the throne be established: and he shall sit upon it in truth in the tabernacle of David, judging, and seeking judgment, and hasting righteousness.

Ecclesiastes 2:1-26

[1] I said in mine heart, go to now, I will prove thee with mirth, therefore enjoy pleasure: and, behold, this also is vanity. [2] I said of laughter, it is mad: and of mirth, What doeth it? [3] I sought in mine heart to give myself unto wine, yet acquainting mine heart with wisdom; and to lay hold on folly, till I might see what was that good for the sons of men, which they should do under the heaven...

Psalm 6:1-10

[1] O Lord, rebuke me not in thine anger, neither chasten me in thy hot displeasure. [2] Have mercy upon me, O Lord; for I am weak: O Lord, heal me; for my bones are vexed. [3] My soul is also, sore vexed: but thou,

O Lord, how long? [4] Return, O Lord, deliver my soul: oh, save me for thy mercies' sake. [5] For in death there is no...

Revelation 21:5

[5] And he that sat upon the throne said, Behold, I make all things new. And he said unto me, write: for these words are true and faithful.

Revelation 20:9

[9] And they went up on the breadth of the earth, and compassed the camp of the saints about, and the beloved city: and fire came down from God out of heaven, and devoured them.

Matthew 5:12-22

[12] Rejoice, and be exceeding glad: for great is your reward in heaven: for so persecuted they the prophets which were before you. [13] Ye are the salt of the earth: but if the salt has lost his savour, wherewith shall it be salted? it is thenceforth good for nothing, but to be

cast out, and to be trodden under foot of men. [14] Ye are the light of the world. A city that is set on a hill cannot be hid.

Matthew 1:15

[15] And Eliud begat Eleazar; and Eleazar begat Matthan; and Matthan begat Jacob;

Amos 9:11-15

[11] In that day will I raise up the tabernacle of David that is fallen, and close up the breaches thereof; and I will raise up his ruins, and I will build it as in the days of old: [12] That they may possess the remnant of Edom, and of all the heathen, which are called by my name, saith the Lord that doeth this. [13] Behold, the days come, saith the Lord, that the plowman shall overtake the reaper, ...

Zechariah 14:8

[8] And it shall be in that day, that living waters shall go out from Jerusalem; half of them toward the former

sea, and half of them toward the hinder sea: in summer and in winter shall it be.

Isaiah 35:1-10

[1] The wilderness and the solitary place shall be glad for them; and the desert shall rejoice, and blossom as the rose. [2] It shall blossom abundantly, and rejoice even with joy and singing: the glory of Lebanon shall be given unto it, the excellency of Carmel and Sharon, they shall see the glory of the Lord, and the excellency of our God. [3] Strengthen ye the weak hands, and confirm the feeble ...

Jeremiah 23:5-6

[5] Behold, the days come, saith the Lord, that I will raise unto David a righteous Branch, and a King shall reign and prosper, and shall execute judgment and justice in the earth. [6] In his days Judah shall be saved, and Israel shall dwell safely: and this is his name whereby he shall be called, The Lord Our Righteousness.

Revelation 2:26-27

^{26} And he that overcometh, and keepeth my works unto the end, to him will I give power over the nations: ^{27} And he shall rule them with a rod of iron; as the vessels of a potter shall they be broken to shivers: even as I received of my Father.

Revelation 11:15

^{15} And the seventh angel sounded; and there were great voices in heaven, saying, the kingdoms of this world are become the kingdoms of our Lord, and of his Christ; and he shall reign for ever and ever.

Acts 1:6

^{6} When they therefore were come together, they asked of him, saying, Lord, wilt thou at this time restore again the kingdom to Israel?

John 18:36

^{36} Jesus answered, my kingdom is not of this world: if my kingdom were of this world, then would my servants fight, that I should not be delivered to the Jews: but now is my kingdom not from hence.

John 14:18

[18] I will not leave you comfortless: I will come to you.

Zechariah 6:12-13

[12] And speak unto him, saying, Thus speaketh the Lord of hosts, saying, Behold the man whose name is The Branch; and he shall grow up out of his place, and he shall build the temple of the Lord: [13] Even he shall build the temple of the Lord; and he shall bear the glory, and shall sit and rule upon his throne; and he shall be a priest upon his throne: and the counsel of peace shall be between them both.

Daniel 9:24-27

[24] Seventy weeks are determined upon thy people and upon thy holy city, to finish the transgression, and to make an end of sins, and to make reconciliation for iniquity, and to bring in everlasting righteousness, and to seal up the vision and prophecy, and to anoint the

most Holy. [25] Know therefore and understand, that from the going forth of the commandment to restore and to build Jerusalem unto the Messiah the Prince shall be...

Revelation 21:1-27

[1] And I saw a new heaven and a new earth: for the first heaven and the first earth were passed away; and there was no more sea. [2] And I John saw the holy city, new Jerusalem, coming down from God out of heaven, prepared as a bride adorned for her husband. [3] And I heard a great voice out of heaven saying, Behold, the tabernacle of God is with men, and he will dwell with them, and they shall be his...

John 14:3

[3] And if I go and prepare a place for you, I will come again, and receive you unto myself; that where I am, there ye may be also.

Ezekiel 44:1-31

[1] Then he brought me back the way of the gate of the outward sanctuary which looketh toward the east; and it was shut. [2] Then said the Lord unto me; This gate shall be shut, it shall not be opened, and no man shall enter in by it; because the Lord, the God of Israel, hath entered in by it, therefore it shall be shut. [3] It is for the prince; the prince, he shall sit in it to eat bread before the ...

Isaiah 51:4-8

[4] Hearken unto me, my people; and give ear unto me, O my nation: for a law shall proceed from me, and I will make my judgment to rest for a light of the people. [5] My righteousness is near; my salvation is gone forth, and mine arms shall judge the people; the isles shall wait upon me, and on mine arm shall they trust. [6] Lift up your eyes to the heavens, and look upon the earth beneath: for the heavens...

Isaiah 66:8

^{8} Who hath heard such a thing? who hath seen such things? Shall the earth be made to bring forth in one day? or shall a nation be born at once? for as soon as Zion travailed, she brought forth her children.

Isaiah 11:6

^{6} The wolf also shall dwell with the lamb, and the leopard shall lie down with the kid; and the calf and the young lion and the fatling together; and a little child shall lead them.

Revelation 21:8

^{8} But the fearful, and unbelieving, and the abominable, and murderers, and whoremongers, and sorcerers, and idolaters, and all liars, shall have their part in the lake which burneth with fire and brimstone: which is the second death.

John 3:16-17

16 For God so loved the world, that he gave his only begotten Son, that whosoever believeth in him should not perish, but have everlasting life. 17 For God sent

not his Son into the world to condemn the world: but that the world through him might be saved.

Chapter 20
May you be enlightened to the
Truth of Jesus Christ

(Yeshua Hamashiach), that will set you free Seeking him Every day, and not just Sundays!

God's (Yahweh's) word says we should strive to be holy as He is holy, and to please remove any idols from our hearts, houses and lives. We are to prioritize our time, be selective about what we watch, be it TV, Movies, YouTube, or your phone, and prioritize your time to read the Bible every day if you can. When I do, I prefer reading the KJV. If another Bible ministers to you and teaches the truth, by all means, read that one. Always pray and ask the Holy Spirit to help you understand and reveal to you in the word what he wants you to know and to provide you with understanding. Seek the Truth while having a relationship with Jesus Christ (Yeshua Hamashiach). The remnant is few; the Lord called us to walk the Narrow Road.

If you have not made Jesus Christ (Yeshua Hamashiach) Lord and Savior of your life, please, I implore you to do so *while there's still time!"

There is an importance of finding and attending a church that teaches strictly the Word of God (Yahweh). I found a couple of YouTube pastors I recommend that are a great source of information: Pastor Robert Breaker, Pastor Sue Keith, and Pastor Naimi Fox, to name a few.

If you can find a church where people gather or a study group teaching the Word of God (Yahweh), please do so! God's (Yahweh's) desire is to have a strong, healthy relationship with you. Part of that is being planted and attending a church regularly if possible. Iron sharpens iron.

When the Beast System is fully intact, the New World Order and One World Religion will be in effect. The mark of the Beast will be issued 3.5 years into the 7 years of Tribulation. Please don't give in and take it. You would be showing allegiance to the Beast, the Antichrist, who will want full worship at that time, and if you choose him over Jesus Christ (Yeshua Hamashiach), you will go to Hell and not Heaven. If you don't have a strong relationship with

Jesus Christ (Yeshua Hamashiach), receive and believe in the Gospel, and repent and renew your relationship with Him now while He can be found. Prepare your hearts, minds, and houses; occupy until Jesus Christ (Yeshua Hamashiach) comes. He'll be here soon enough!

Psalm 23 and Psalm 91 are two **Psalms** that I personally love and recommend everyone learn them especially for the times we are living! They cover everything. My husband reads them out loud every night before we go to bed. We serve an Awesome God and don't forget You have angels that watch over you too!!

Chapter 21
My 2 favorite Psalms covering Everything

Psalm 23

[1] The Lord is my shepherd; I shall not want. [2] He maketh me to lie down in green pastures: he leadeth me beside the still waters. [3] He restoreth my soul: he leadeth me in the paths of righteousness for his name's sake. [4] Yea, though I walk through the valley of the shadow of death, I will fear no evil: for thou art with me; thy rod and thy staff they comfort me. [5] Thou preparest a table before me in the presence of my enemies: thou annointest my head with oil; my cup runneth over. [6] Surely goodness and mercy shall follow me all the days of my life: and I will dwell in the house of the Lord forever. Amen.

Psalm 91

^{1} He that dwelleth in the secret place of the most-High shall abide under the shadow of the Almighty. ^{2} I will say of the Lord, He is my refuge and my fortress: my God; in him will I trust. ^{3} Surely, he shall deliver thee from the snare of the fowler, and from the noisome pestilence. ^{4} He shall cover thee with his feathers, and under his wings shalt thou trust: his truth shall be thy shield and buckler. ^{5} Thou shalt not be afraid for the terror by night; nor for the arrow that flieth by day; ^{6} Nor for the pestilence that walketh in darkness; nor for the destruction that wasteth at noonday. ^{7} A thousand shall fall at thy side, and ten thousand at thy right hand; but it shall not come nigh thee. ^{8} Only with thine eyes shalt thou behold and see the reward of the wicked. ^{9} Because thou hast made the Lord, which is my refuge, even the most- High, thy habitation; ^{10} There shall no evil befall thee, neither shall any plague come nigh thy dwelling. ^{11} For he shall give his angels charge over thee, to keep thee in all thy ways. ¹² They shall bear thee up in their hands, lest thou dash thy foot against a stone. ¹³ Thou shalt tread upon the lion and adder: the young lion and the dragon shalt thou trample under feet. ¹⁴ Because he hath set his love upon me, therefore will I deliver him: I will set him on high, because he hath known my name. ¹⁵ He shall call upon me, and I will answer him: I will be with him in trouble; I will deliver him, and honour him. ¹⁶ With long life will I satisfy him, and shew him my salvation. Amen.

Chapter 22
Blood Moons

Bible prophecy experts teach:

Blood Moons are tied to events that affect Israel.

Blood Moons begin in Tragedy and end up in Triumph.

We have a Blood Moon on Monday sundown, March 2, 2026

into Tuesday nightfall, March 3, 2026

The next Tetrad of Blood Moons occurs in 2032 and 2033

Exactly 2000 years after the death and resurrection of Jesus Christ.

The First 2 Tetrads occur on **April 25** and **October 18** of **2032.**

The Last 2 Tetras occur on Passover, **April 14, 2033**

And on Sukkot, **October 8, 2033** (Jewish Holidays)

The total Solar Eclipse is on **March 30, 2033**

Scriptures are referenced from the King James Version and from the Ancient Text by George M. Lamsa's translation.

I have quite a few Bibles, different versions, and personally like reading from the KJV bible including the 1611 KJV that includes the Apocrypha. I've read a few scriptures from a little of The Holy Bible and from the Ancient Text by George M. Lamsas. Translation, as well as the complete Ethiopian Bible in English.

If you'd like to purchase a King James Version (KJV) Bible or

The Holy Bible: from the Ancient Text by George M. Lamsa's Translation

You have several options:

Where to purchase a KJV Bible, or a Bible of your choice!

Online Access: You can access the King James Bible online through the King James Bible Online website, which provides the Authorized King James Version (KJV) of the Bible.

Purchasing Options: You can buy either Bible from various retailers, including Amazon and the KJV store.

Free Downloads: If you prefer a digital version, you can download the King James Version from the KJV Bible.

Mobile Apps: You can also find mobile apps for the King James platforms, like Google Play.

In the back of a KJV Bible, there is an Index, a Dictionary of Scripture Proper Names, Subject – Index, Concordance, and Maps that help you on your journey in day-by-day learning about our Heavenly Father God's (Yahweh) word. There is usually a Dictionary of Scripture Proper Names found together with compendious references to some of the Principal Incidents connected with the persons and places mentioned in Holy Scripture.

May Our Heavenly Father, God, Yahweh, bless you and keep you. May the LORD make his face shine upon thee, and be gracious unto thee: The LORD lift up his countenance upon thee, and give thee peace. Amen.

May you be filled with the Holy Spirit, and may your eyes be opened to discern the times we are living in. We are living in the last days. The most important thing to do is to put your faith and trust in the finished work of Jesus Christ (Yeshua Hamashiach) who is God (Yahweh) in the flesh. He took our sinful nature and paid for our sins so we don't have to pay for them in hell. He shed his blood for us on that cross. Make Jesus Christ (Yeshua Hamashiach) Lord and Savior of your life if he isn't already. He loves you, will provide for you, and will direct your path when you put your full trust in him alone. Cast your cares upon Jesus Christ (Yeshua Hamashiach); He is a prayer away! Amen.

About the Author
Courtney Lande

Courtney Lande's life would not exist, nor would anything, if it weren't for Jesus Christ (Yeshua Hamashiach), as He is her rock and shelter in the storms of life. She owes everything she is and has to Him, her best friend and love of her life, who means the world to her, as Jesus Christ (Yeshua Hamashiach) gets all glory, honor, and praise for everything he is and stands for.

When she's not sharing the Gospel (good news) and love of Jesus Christ (Yeshua Hamashiach) and the Kingdom of God (Yahushua), she can be found going to thrift stores with her husband and afterwards stopping for coffee or chai at BLOOM on the way home, a favorite she loves to do on her way home from shopping. Writing poetry and songs and dancing are her first loves. She likes a clean, organized home where she will cook and make up recipes as she goes. She loves to can, be it meat, veggies, or garden; loves music; and loves to sing! Researching the hidden things of this world is of major interest, and listening to various podcasts, be it from YouTube or the radio, is as well.

"Normal"
isn't Coming back
But Jesus is!

Did you know that Jesus Christ, whose true name is Yeshua Hamashiach, was put to death on a device made by the Romans, a cross, an upright wooden beam that formed a T-shaped structure, around 33 A.D.? He was handed over to the Roman authorities after being betrayed by Judas Iscariot and accused of blasphemy and being King of the Jews. He endured severe beatings and mockery before being nailed to the cross at the place of the skull, also known as Golgotha. For approximately 6 hours, he hung on the cross, and while he hung there dying, he expressed love and forgiveness toward those who were torturing him.

Jesus Christ (Yeshua Hamashiach) took on the sins of humanity, offering redemption and the gift of eternal life. His death was God's plan for salvation as he fulfilled the Old Testament prophecies. This was not only a historical event but also a transformative act, allowing believers to have a relationship with our Heavenly Father, God (Yahweh).

Jesus led a life of example filled with grace, love, and sacrifice. His death represents divine love, justice, and the hope of salvation for all who believe, have faith, and trust in the word of God. When you make Jesus Christ (Yeshua Hamashiach) your personal Lord and Savior by surrendering to His Authority, committing to live according to His will, and honoring Him in all aspects of life, His Authority is foundational to the Christian life.

We are saved and justified by the blood of Jesus Christ (Yeshua Hamashiach) the moment we make Him our personal Lord and Savior, believing in His blood atonement for us. We are saved and justified by the blood of Jesus (Yeshua). It is having an intimate relationship with him birthed out of sincerity and humility.

In a world of uncertainty, over 2000+ Biblical prophecies have come to pass and are unfolding at a rate faster than a moving freight train. The signs of the end times are everywhere as we are living out the last days. Our dollar is losing its value every day; we are watching AI be implemented everywhere, digital ID, and QR codes that track your every move. This information is out there and will apply to everyone, whether you're Republican or Democrat, no matter the party; what's taking place is all biblical and had been prophesied long ago. A tyrannical New World Order government will form under the Antichrist (Beast) of Revelation, lasting for 7 years. Unless the time is shortened, no flesh will be saved, for this will be the worst time in history.

There will be an Antichrist, what the Bible calls the Beast, who will take control of the Beast system and sit in the rebuilt 3rd Temple in Jerusalem, declaring himself God and wanting to be worshipped. Jesus (Yeshua) is coming back for his own in what's called a "Harpazo" (in Greek) rapture, a snatching of believers, including both Christians and Jews. There is a total of 7 raptures in the Biblical Scriptures. 3 happened at the beginning of time, and the last 4 will take place around the time of Tribulation, as I provide scriptures throughout this book to back up any and all Biblical claims. We are not appointed to wrath, as Jesus says throughout scripture, to look and watch for him. The last time he comes, he comes with his Saints (the Believers, including both Jew and Gentile) to the Battle of Armageddon. He will also gather the nations and pour out his fierce anger upon the wicked, as the earth will be devoured by fire. He will end this tyranny and start his reign as king on the new earth with his new bride!

We all need to confess any sins daily to get right with Jesus Christ (Yeshua Hamashiach): believe me, you don't want to be here and get left behind when this period of time comes, and it'll be here sooner than you think!

Let's give God (Yehusha) Jesus Christ (Yeshua Hamashiach) all Glory, Honor, and Praise for everything!!!

Made in the USA

2026